APPRECIATIVE LEADERSHIP

JACK RICCHIUTO

DesigningLife Books

APPRECIATIVE LEADERSHIP

DesigningLife Books 2005

DesigningLife Books
PO Box 15421
Cleveland OH 44115
216.373.7475
www.DesigningLife.com

For book orders, workshops, and coaching based on the book, contact
Jack Ricchiuto / orders@designinglife.com / 216.373.7475 (EST)
Visit the book's website: www.AppreciativeLeadership.org

Ricchiuto, Jack, 1952 –
    Appreciative Leadership / Jack Ricchiuto

    ISBN: 0-9661703-5-0

        1.   Leadership.   2. Organization development.

            I.   Title.

First edition, Paperback, November 2004

Cover Design: Tia Andrako
Cover Photo: Ellen Shafer
Production: BookMasters, Mansfield OH 44905

APPRECIATIVE LEADERSHIP

THE APPRECIATIVE LEADERSHIP MANIFESTO

1. We want to honor the resources people bring to their work as deeply as we honor the resources of the earth.
2. We want to do business in a way that supports abundance rather than scarcity.
3. We want to understand that the sustainability of any community depends on its capacity for appreciation.
4. We want to base our performance on what we appreciate rather than what we fear
5. We want to visualize a community of work that's organized by its capabilities and opportunities.
6. We want to define leadership as those who take the lead with a radically appreciative focus.
7. We want to trust in our happiness as a more sustainable motivator than our unhappiness.
8. We want to spend more time measuring that which we want to increase than what we want to decrease.
9. We want to make business decisions in ways that serve this generation and those to follow.
10. We want appreciative organizations that support local living economies
11. We want appreciative leaders who seek the optimum rather than maximum or minimum
12. We want to respect the profound differences between leadership and management in the growth of an organization.
13. We want leaders who have durable faith in the seen and unseen capabilities of their people.
14. We want to fill leadership positions with people who have leadership capabilities.
15. We want to trust people's innate appreciation for order in their work.
16. We want to ask people to base their work on their dreams for the best outcomes possible.
17. We want people to bring all of their strengths to their work.
18. We want people to understand the depth and breadth of their strengths.
19. We want to understand our "weaknesses" as strengths used at the wrong time
20. We want to awaken in everyone their capacity for passion in their work.
21. We want to create alignment between our passions and the passions of our markets.

22. We want to understand the role of knowledge in a wholistic way.
23. We want to translate our passions into measurable performance targets.
24. We want our passions to move us beyond the boundaries of our comfort zones.
25. We want to hold people accountable for understanding their successes and the causes of their successes.
26. We want to help everyone see that success is about the transfer of existing strengths to new situations.
27. We want to help everyone understand that they already have what it takes to succeed.
28. We want to understand that success is about alignment.
29. We want to grow communities of work that empower people with a sustainable sense of self-confidence.
30. We want to engage in work that honors our limitations.
31. We want to create organizations on the understanding that organizations are always self-organizing whether we see them that way or not.
32. We want leaders to be in constant search and creation of new opportunities to help people manifest their personal and shared capabilities.
33. We want to totally reinvent how we define and deal with outcomes we call "failure."
34. We want leaders who are passionate about the efforts and achievements of others.
35. We want leaders who are present, proactive, creative, and dependable.
36. We want organizations designed to allow everyone to share in networks of leadership.
37. We want to have a deep understanding of the strengths of those we hire.
38. We want strengths-based performance feedback that inspires and empowers.
39. We want to understand that turnover is inevitable and base it on the growth of people.
40. We want to support people's continuous growth with mentoring and coaching.
41. We want to base our ability to differentiate ourselves in our market on our ability to value the uniqueness of our people.
42. We want leaders whose use of time aligns with their passions and strengths and those of the organization.
43. We want leaders who are skillful facilitators of appreciative consensus.

44. We want leaders who thrive on change.
45. We want leaders who are more passionate about collaboration than hierarchy.
46. We want leaders who are good at virally infecting people with passion through skillful and appreciative storytelling.
47. We want leaders who do enough self-care to sustain strong energy levels through times of challenge.
48. We want leaders whose appreciation at work is simply an expression of an entire lifestyle of appreciation.
49. We want to design every aspect of organizations from an intention to unleash passions, strengths, and opportunities.
50. We want leaders who know how to foster a culture of appreciation.
51. We want leaders who help people practice self-appreciation in everything.
52. We want strengths-based teams.
53. We want organizations known for creating entrepreneurs.
54. We want organizations that foster informal environments to cultivate their rich network of relationships.
55. We want to base continuous improvement opportunities on the passions and strengths of people.
56. We want to understand that partnership relationships outperform customer-supplier relationships.
57. We want to create learning organizations.
58. We want to create micro-communities where learning can thrive.
59. We want to continuously cultivate the next generation of appreciative leadership.
60. We want to expect that appreciative organizations have unlimited potential.

Sign the Manifesto @ www.AppreciativeLeadership.org

THE APPRECIATIVE CHALLENGE

We live in a universe that reveals itself according to the lens we use to experience it.

If we expect to see abundance, the world reveals itself as abundant. If we expect to see deficiency, the world appears deficient. The lens we bring to our life and our work has profound impact on the way we experience our world.

What we pay attention to expands to fill the space of our everyday experience. Whether we've been inspired by the last century of quantum physics or by spiritual teachings over the past 50,000 years, the message is clear: *The scope of our life is shaped by the focus of our attention.*

Our personal lens is often a reflection of the collective lens. Our sense of belonging invites us to see the world the way others in our communities see it. And because our perspectives are rooted in our communities, these communities have a profound social responsibility to inspire the highest level of value and impact for ourselves and the generations to follow.

The two kinds of communities that have the most significant influence on our worldview are our communities of *place* and *purpose*.

Communities of place include the people with whom we share a house, a neighborhood, and a local region. Communities of purpose include the people with whom we share passions, resources, projects, learning, enterprises, and trade. Businesses, schools, communities of faith and spiritual practice, non-profits, associations, cooperatives, and public organizations are communities of purpose.

Because we spend such a significant part of our lives there, our communities of work have a unique and significant responsibility to inspire and support an appreciative perspective. The communities that are the most life-giving are those that are the most appreciative.

Appreciative organizations focus on *what they have and want, what's working, and why.* In these organizations, people feel inspired and engaged. Appreciation is a lens that inspires passions, reveals opportunities, and engages strengths. Appreciation connects them to the core of their being where passion emerges. It focuses them on opportunities rather than constraints.

Deficiency focused organizations attend to what they *don't have, don't want, what's not working, and why.* People in these organizations elevate complaining, whining, and criticizing to an art form. No achievement is ever good enough to eclipse the problem-focus that dominates and distorts people's consciousness.

Luckily, more communities are moving from a base of deficiency to one of appreciation. This radical shift from a deficiency lens to an appreciative lens requires a whole new vocabulary. It requires a new manifesto, social aesthetic, and set of questions to inspire and energize new conversations. It requires faith that being appreciative is a more sustainable attitude than a deficiency approach.

This shift will not happen quickly or easily. According to the Gallup Organization, about 20% of 1.7 million employees surveyed globally feel that their organizations make good use of their strengths in their work.

This statistic is profoundly ironic in an age where no organization would let 80% of their non-people resources go unused or wasted on a daily basis. Leaving money on the table is an unsustainable strategy for any organization, however it defines its highest purpose and mission.

The practice of wasted resources is rooted in organizations that still maintain deficiency models of leadership that focus on people's performance problems, gaps, and weaknesses. Obsession with what's wrong prevents attention to the organization's strengths and kills whatever passion people are capable of in their work. This model is the fastest way for an organization to join the unfortunate trend of resource wasters.

Over the past quarter century of coaching leaders and teams in organizations, I've been struck with how easy it is for some cultures to be engaging and inspiring, while others find it just as easy to be fearful and controlling. Working across a diverse mix of industries, I continue to encounter organizations still dominated by deficiency perspectives. In every case, my passion is to help people move individually and collectively along the continuum toward greater appreciation.

Deficiency focused organizations struggle every day as they try to move forward while applying the accelerator of goals *and* the breaks of a deficiency perspective. They burn a lot of energy and spin a lot of wheels without always move quickly or successfully in the direction of their deepest desires. Operating from the only model they tend to know, they do the best they can until they discover alternatives.

I am amazed at our human capacity for making life harder and more complicated than it is. The lure of being problem-obsessed tempts us to go through our work, our life, and our relationships with white knuckles and gritted teeth, believing that gain requires pain. This self-fulfilling expectation only prevents us from experiencing a more sustainable and life-giving appreciation of what we have, what we do, and who we are.

The good news is that we don't have to change who we are to become more of what we can be. We simply need to be more appreciative about who we are and how we discover and create new ways of being together.

An appreciative model of leadership views people's passions and strengths as their greatest opportunities for organizational success. The appreciative priority starts with knowing people's capabilities and aligning them with the organization's most rewarding market opportunities. Appreciative leadership drives the sustainability of the organization where people are not the problem; they are the solution. Appreciative leadership works because it empowers people to do their adaptive best in a world of dynamic and complex opportunities.

It's the job of appreciative leader to focus people's attention in ways that inspire passion, discover opportunities, and engage strengths. How to develop a culture of appreciative leadership is the challenge of this century. It is also the focus of this book's invitation and conversation.

1. THE NEW RESPECT FOR RESOURCES

We want to honor the resources people bring to their work as deeply as we honor the resources of the earth.

Fast realizing that we live by the grace of our resources, we're discovering that everything we experience and achieve, discover, and enjoy in life and work comes about thanks to a vast and abundant universe of resources. We breathe with the air the earth gives us, we perform with the information people give us, and we learn from the knowledge experience gives us. We connect with the people our community gives us. Without our resources, nothing is possible.

To live in deep and creative appreciation of our resources is the basis of being whole and vital, individually and collectively. As long as we have the lens to see it, we live and work and play in a universe of abundant resources.

This generation is a generation engaged in cultivating unprecedented dimensions of appreciation for our resources. We are sensitive to the non-local impact of how we use our resources. We're more dedicated than ever to a resource efficiency that leads to wise use, reuse, and regeneration of the resources we have.

This new level of respect is both modern and ancient. Best of all, we're moving toward appreciating what people bring to the table of their communities of place and purpose. We're daily committing ourselves to a more wholistic appreciation for all of our resources, especially the renewable resources of our skills and knowledge that have no limit to their potential uses.

- *What would your organization be like if the resources people bring to the table were treated as important as the capital and financial resources of the organization?*

2. ABUNDANCE/SCARCITY

We want to do business in a way that supports abundance rather than scarcity.

An appreciative perspective is an abundance perspective. It's based on the observation that we live in a world of more resources than we can ever use in a lifetime.

We now know that we have more renewable resources like sun, water, and wind power than we need to power the planet forever. We have more cultivatable land and ecologically wise technologies than we need to feed the planet many times over.

We have more books to read, music and poetry to hear, art to see, and theatre performances to attend than we could ever have time to enjoy. We have more beautiful and awesome places to visit than we could ever visit. We have more stories to tell, poems to write, songs to sing, and recipes to try than we could ever have the opportunity to experience in a single lifespan.

Just having this perspective grounds us in durable and tangible optimism about having the resources we need to succeed in our communities. It is a view that inspires us to collaborate with rather than compete against others with whom we share this abundant world. It invites us to work with rather than fight against everyone else with whom we share the resources of this planet. It encourages us to do business in a way that allows other businesses to grow and thrive in complementary and synergistic ways.

- *What new dreams might your organization be capable of dreaming if it believed that it had access to unlimited natural and people resources?*

The deficiency perspective is grounded in a scarcity mentality. It comes from a belief that there is not enough to go around, that we must view others as combative competitors in a world where there can only be a limited number of winners around the scarcity pie. Feeling like we never have enough, never do enough, and never are enough is less a statement about the world's abundance and more about our beliefs in a world we fail to see accurately.

The quantum, self-fulfilling side of the equation is that the world appears to be more abundant or deficient depending on how we tend to interact with it. Beliefs inspire behavior and behavior is destiny. Scarcity beliefs are self-fulfilling.

Appreciative leaders resonate from an attitude of abundance and as a result naturally see more resources available than their deficiency perspective neighbors. Appreciative leaders seek forgiveness more than permission and take more initiative than they often have permission for. If they're operating in declining markets or industries, they get creative about new ways to use their resources and expand their resources to create new markets. They're interested in new synergies of improvements and innovations precisely because they believe in the abundance of resources and opportunities.

3. SUSTAINABLE COMMUNITIES

We want to understand that the sustainability of any community depends on its capacity for appreciation.

One of the natural outgrowths of this renaissance of abundance consciousness is appreciation for sustainable communities.

Whether they're work, faith, family, social, or civic communities, sustainable communities are marked by their *enduring commitment to using this generation's resources in ways that will provide the most value for generations to follow.*

This attention to the next generation is not an arrogantly patriarchal or colonistic intention to decide what their world will be like. It is about creating a world that gives next generations the greatest flexibility in shaping their most life-giving choices.

• *What might your organization's vision include if it went out at least 20 years - that it might not include if it was confined to only the next 2 quarters or 2 years?*

Communities of work become unsustainable to the degree that they focus more on people's deficiencies, gaps, and failures than their passions, strengths, and accomplishments. The focus on deficiencies prevents communities from fully understanding and leveraging people's strengths in their work and their life. A community's movement toward sustainability is shaped by its movement toward overt and robust appreciation for its rich and dynamic field of passions and strengths.

4. THE TRADITIONAL DEFICIENCY MODEL

We want to base our performance on what we appreciate rather than what we fear.

Many traditionally-structured organizations operate from deficiency models of performance. In this model, everything is a problem to be solved. Customers and clients are problems to be solved by employees; employees are problems to be solved my managers; managers are problems to be solved by employees.

The deficiency model focuses on *what's wrong* with people and things in the community -- what's missing, what we want to avoid, reduce, downsize, prevent, eliminate, and cut -- the gaps, weaknesses, fears, and flaws.

Every perspective we have in life is shaped by the language forming it. The language of the deficiency model is always some variation on three themes: 1) we live in a world of problems in which, 2) resources are scarce, and so 3) we need to compete against others in our community of practice to survive.

Because a deficiency focus filters out what's good in favor of obsessing over what's wrong, deficiency managers can often ignore or take for granted good performers in the organization. They make the mistake of investing valuable time pushing the motivational string of the lowest performers instead of pulling more value from the passions and strengths of middle and higher performers. In the worst scenarios, they ask less of their poorer performers because their cynical obsession with weaknesses and problems blinds them to unutilized and uncovered capabilities.

A deficiency perspective makes us increasingly pessimistic about people's capabilities because we're not discovering and using them. Unless an appreciative counter-culture emerges, pessimism turns into cynicism and the whole downward spiral becomes predictably self-fulfilling and self-reinforcing.

People know when they work for deficiency organizations. Praise is rare, good performers feel unappreciated, and people feel micromanaged or unsupported. Achievements go largely taken for granted and uncelebrated. Restrictions exceed permissions and the excessive layers of management make innovation and fun unlikely. If the culture attracts enough deficiency people, no one questions that things could be otherwise. The deficiency focus creates ideal conditions for a culture of blame, denial, finger-pointing, accountability-projecting, and excuse-making.

In deficiency organizations, people have all kinds of capabilities that go largely unknown, unrecognized, and unused. People don't feel like their best is utilized and appreciated. When it comes to resources, deficiency managers feel chronically deprived.

- *What kind of personal passions and strengths in your organization might elude the eyes of deficiency managers?*

The focus on deficiencies puts a priority on managers always chasing the tails of problems. Spending most of their time on reactive fire-fighting, they rarely feel able to be proactive enough to prevent the cycles of problems they need to react to, fight against, and drown in. A deficiency perspective breeds only more of the same in a cycle that cannot end itself.

5. WHY THE DEFICIENCY MODEL DOESN'T WORK

We want to visualize a community of work that's organized by its capabilities and opportunities.

The problem with the problem focus is that it feels and functions like treading water in an undertow. The fundamental operating belief behind the deficiency model is that if we don't focus on what's wrong, chaos will reign. According to this mythology, our obsession with what's wrong is the royal road to performance excellence.

People raised in deficiency cultures tend to perpetuate the model, not as much out of passion for pain, but out of a lack of alternatives otherwise. The deficiency belief is a toxic and alluring illusion that continues to squelch appreciation for our passion and strengths.

Most organizations perpetuate, promote, and tolerate the model because they still believe that inattention to what's wrong is at the core of failure on all scales. In deficiency cultures, there is always a lurking mythology that suffering in life is inevitable, especially when we go after what we want. In the gospel according to deficiencies, our worst performers, nastiest customers, and most despised suppliers keep disappointing us precisely because they don't pay enough attention to what's wrong.

- *How do people express a deep desire for appreciation in their work?*

But the more time I spend with these people who chronically and acutely disappoint the performance standard bearers, the more I discover that these are some of the more negative people you can ever meet on the planet. *All they focus on is what's wrong*. They are masters of the negative obvious, believing that fear and sacrifice are more intelligent motivators than love. All their deficiency focus does is make them cranky, difficult, and change-phobic.

The deficiency vexation also leaves people increasingly dispassionate. And the costs to compensate the deficiency drain on personal meaning through extrinsic incentives are bottomless. It doesn't help that deficiency communities excel in the practice of institutional entitlement programs that only perpetuate learned helplessness. Over time, deficiency organizations put themselves at risk of extinction as their compensation costs become unsustainable.

The deficiency perspective demoralizes people and has never proven to efficiently improve performance in a sustainable and meaningful way. Few people walk around organizations feeling happier now that someone has taken the time to focus them on what's not right today and why. In deficiency cultures, without engagement, people seek entitlement. Without passion, people seek position. Without appreciation, people seek to avoid responsibility in every creative way possible.

The deficiency model fails to inspire and engage people simply because it focuses us on what we don't have - what's missing.

Moving away from or against something we don't want is a non-sustainable and ultimately unfulfillable posture. The only way we move forward is moving toward rather than against - focusing on what we want *more* rather than what we want *less*. The deficiency model's insistence that we obsess on our weaknesses and failures distracts and prevents us from obsessing on our capabilities, and makes us vulnerable to not improving our performance in ways we can.

People discover they perform better not because they've obsessed on their weaknesses but because they've become better able to utilize their strengths.

6. THE APPRECIATIVE MODEL

We want to define leadership as those who take the lead with a radically appreciative focus.

The role of an appreciative leader is to inspire passion, identify opportunities, and engage the strengths of people in the community.

The appreciative model is a focus on what's *right* rather than what's wrong. It's a shameless and unhesitant passion about what's *working*, what we *want*, what we *have* to work with, and what's *going well and why*. It's a focus on our resources, opportunities, networks of relationships, our passions and the passions of our communities and value ecologies.

The role of appreciative leader is to believe in and tap into the core goodness of people. It is coming from a place of expectation that people tend to do their best when the best is expected.

- *Do you think it's possible for people to believe in the natural goodness of other people before they believe in their own natural goodness?*

People are inspired to do their best work when they can see a compelling relationship between their passions and the passions of the community. They are energized in a sustainable way when they understand the relationship between their capabilities and the requirements of their work. People do their best caring and thinking, innovating and collaborating when they believe that their community deeply respects their strengths as valued natural resources to be used and reused for sustainability.

The appreciative model is based on the belief that we perform at our best when we focus on achieving the highest standards of outcomes with the best we have to offer. Optimum personal, team, and community performance occurs when we're using our capabilities in ways that create sustainable value for this generation and those to follow.

The appreciative approach is an aesthetic. Rather than talking about what's wrong and what we don't want and feeling intimidated or frustrated, we rivet our attention on the reality of what we do want and the conditions required to bring that reality about. It is a totally positive approach that has little room for obsessing over the negative.

When appreciative leaders spend their time obsessing about what's good rather than what's bad, it is far from a denial of what needs improvement. Appreciative leaders allow themselves to be guided by the highest levels of dreams and standards possible. Their approach to continuous improvement is based on leveraging strengths rather than eliminating weaknesses.

From an appreciative perspective, there is no value in calling what we haven't yet achieved a weakness, or see it as something wrong to correct, a problem to solve, or a gap to eliminate. We can master every sport, speak 14 languages, and win international prizes in a dozen fields and even if we live a hundred years beyond today, we will still have a thousand things we haven't yet achieved, skills we still don't have, and knowledge we lack.

In an appreciative sense, everything unachieved is simply an opportunity space of possibility - an opportunity to discover new uses of what we have in order to manifest what we want.

People like to work in appreciative communities because they prefer a positive approach. They like working with leaders who empower, inspire, and engage rather than criticize and coerce. They find they naturally perform at higher levels with a sense of esteem, respect, and confidence.

7. THE MYTH OF APPRECIATION

We want to trust in our happiness as a more sustainable motivator than our unhappiness.

Many communities hardwire each new generation with the belief that if we appreciate ourselves "too much", we will render ourselves inert with self-acceptance. As strenuously as we strive for happiness, we irrationally resist its lure as the root of apathy.

The underlying belief at work: *If we're happy with ourselves and our world, we won't have the motivation to change or improve it.* The dysfunctional corollary is simple and at the root of much of our needless suffering: *we must maintain some measure of unhappiness in order to be motivated for change.*

Luckily, brave souls in every generation and organization continue to challenge these beliefs, discovering the grand paradox that being happy is not an inevitable barrier to noticing or acting on opportunities for improvement. In fact, the more appreciative we are in life, the more creativity we have to notice opportunities and the more confidence we have in our capacity for innovating with our capabilities.

Ironically, *the happier we are with ourselves, the more energy we have for change.* When we're at our happiest, we are most keenly conscious of and confident in our resources and assets, capabilities and passions, opportunities and strengths.

Our happiness gives us the energy that is typically and dependably depleted by criticizing ourselves for being deficient and then needing to develop various remedies to quiet this pain. Happiness creates the inner quiet it takes for us to be collaborative, creative, and aware of new opportunities for putting our talents to work. Customers reward happy providers with more loyalty, making the organization more successful in the short term and more sustainable in the long term.

Unhappiness makes us deficiency focused in a way that blinds us to noticing new opportunities and remembering the rich ecology of our strengths. Unhappiness turns our focus and interest to the small self; happiness directs us to see beyond to our larger selves. Happiness connects us to the same degree that unhappiness disconnects us.

- *How much more do you think your organization could accomplish if people every day came from a place of feeling happy with themselves and their organization?*

What more efficiently inspires and engages us is interacting with new people and new ideas in our communities, dreaming new and larger dreams, and translating these into actionable targets. What more sustainably energizes us is paying attention to and inventing new opportunities that call forth new ways for us to use our personal and collective strengths and resources.

With new intentions for a new future, we can be as happy with ourselves and our world as we can possibly be. We don't need to fear excess happiness. If millions of us on the planet were happier beyond what our imaginations can conjure, we would still have an infinite number of opportunities to bring happiness to millions of others in this generation, not to mention the next. Bottom line: *we can stand to be as happy as we want.*

8. THE METRICS OF SUSTAINABILITY

We want to spend more time measuring that which we want to increase than what we want to decrease.

One of the core differentiating values of appreciative communities is that they operate from a different set of metrics.

In deficiency organizations, we obsess over defect rates and customer complaints, variances and variations, losses, turnover, waste, violations, and costs. We take people away from their work to glaze over deficiency charts and cower over deficiency graphs. We maintain an unfortunate and self-defeating culture by reminding people where they're falling short quarter after quarter. We use naïve reward and recognition systems to divide people into winners and losers.

Appreciative organizations dutifully measure deficiency indicators when they are obligated by deficiency focused regulatory, credentialing, and governance entities.

But where they put most conversational emphasis and public celebration is on the *appreciative* side of life. They promote conversations dominated by what's going right, what's improving, and what's been achieved - *and why*. They spend time measuring performance against appreciative standards - what the organization wants more of rather than less of. They measure and communicate the number of satisfied customers and why, the number of products produced to standard and why, the number of successful projects and why.

If what gets measured gets done, measuring our success is critical to promoting it. Arriving at new levels of success next quarter and year follows riding on the waves of this term's successes, not failures. People take the risks of change and improvement when they have upward spiraling confidence in their ability to improvise and perform. Success breeds success.

What we measure depends on the questions that organize our formal and informal conversations. In appreciative organizations, leaders are constantly inquiring about the kind of impact we want to create beyond the obvious obstacles and challenges we face. They're continuously asking people to report on what's improving today, this week, this quarter, and this year.

Deficiency is the politics of *decrease*; appreciation is the currency of *increase*. Appreciative leaders are always measuring for the baseline of good performance so they can assess the direction and tempo of improvement.

- *What are 20 things you'd like to see more of in your work and organization?*

To a large degree, it's a matter of emphasis and perspective. In a deficiency oriented culture, growth is framed as decreasing the empty half of the glass half empty. In appreciative cultures, growth is framed as increasing the full half of the glass.

The distinction is far from superficial. It totally drives the tone and viral attitude of the organization's culture. On a practical level, any goal and standard can be framed and measured in terms of what we want more of rather than less of. At the end of the day, we tend to get more of whatever we measure for.

9. SUSTAINABLE VISION

We want to make business decisions in ways that serve this generation and those to follow.

It takes little wattage of consciousness to notice how change is a constant in our communities of work. As much as we try to surprise-proof our organizations with unbending rules, roles, and rituals, the more unpredictability, uncertainty, and ambiguity continues to reign.

Even given the constancy of change, sustained purpose can be a compelling and enduring guide to creating sustainable communities of work.

One of the prime tasks of appreciative leaders is making sure today's performance impacts the community long after today's leaders move on in their lives and careers. Appreciative leaders care how this generation's choices impact the choices of the next generation. They care how resources are developed today in ways that shape the possibilities of performance in the future. They care about the legacy they leave the next generation of leaders and members of their community of work.

Sustainable organizations are dedicated to knowing how the choices they make today open up and close off options for future generations.

- *What kind of choices and options do you want the next generation in your organization to have thanks to the choices your organization makes today?*

Organizations don't know where their markets will be in 3 years; they don't know exactly what their value ecologies will look like 2 years from now. They don't know the mix of new resources hired in and developed in the organization 1 year from now.

So how is constancy of purpose possible? We can, even with the infinite field of unknowns, decide what kind of difference we want our organization to make in the future. We can decide this year that we will be dedicated to the organization's capacity for impacting economic development in its local region. We can decide that we will produce only what best serves the ecology and the lifestyles of the members of our organization.

We can decide that our organization will become a more vibrant contributor to the schools in our markets. We can dedicate resources to helping the people in our organization thrive in their personal lives and communities. We can decide to create an entrepreneurial organization that becomes known for spinning off new entrepreneurial initiatives.

We can make sure we have sustainable intentions that go out at least 2 and 3 *generations* (rather than years) out. It doesn't matter that these intentions might change and morph in unexpected and unpredictable ways. It only matters that we act today with intentions that represent impact beyond the current generation serving the organization.

As for what exact businesses we'll be in 10 years from now to serve these overarching goals, that will be up to the ever-shifting mix of resources and opportunities that emerge serendipitously and intentionally from our choices and actions today.

10. CIRCLE ECONOMIES

We want appreciative organizations that support circle (local living) economies

Appreciative organizations, in their commitment to sustainability, know that their sustainability interdepends on the sustainability of other local organizations. Businesses depend on schools that depend on parents who depend on businesses.

Local living economies, known in China as *circle economies*, are local economies where organizations intentionally produce what is used locally in ways that continue the value cycle within the local economic habitat. Prosperity recycles within local economies.

The opposite is an economy dominated by organizations that suck value out of local economies, channeling revenues to non-local economies, and draining the local economy of the value it produces.

- *How could your organization be more supportive of its local living economy?*

As raving fans of the local economy, sustainable organizations buy and sell local whenever possible. They give preference to local vendors and partners when contracting for products and services. They partner with local schools for future employees and leaders. They practice social responsibility in volunteering for civic projects whenever they can. They appreciate their local resources as much as they appreciate their own resources.

Appreciative organizations continuously track the resources and capabilities outside their organization, knowing that this consciousness fuels creative collaborations with other organizations, individuals, and communities. They stay on top of what's working and why as another strategy for discovering new partnership opportunities.

11. SEEKING THE OPTIMUM

We want appreciative leaders who seek the optimum rather than maximum or minimum

An unsustainable practice is one based on unsustainable obsession with *more is better*. Our resources and opportunities don't always support more. There is also little validity in an absolute: *less of better*.

In sustainable ecosystems, living systems grow in balance with the rest of their ecological habitats. Optimum growth is growth that supports life in the long run.

- *What would it mean for your organization to seek optimum market share?*

What is the optimum rather than maximum (or minimum) hours people should work in a day or week? What's the optimum level of efforts and outcomes people should strive to reach?

The optimum perspective centers us in an intention to respect the very resources we depend on to achieve what we want. It invites us to use our resources in a renewable way. Optimum is not always maximum. It is not always the most; it's just enough to get the job done while allowing us to have resources for the future.

Many organizations have embraced the anorexic strategy of less is more. This can be a disguised version of deficiency and scarcity. Excess efficiency burns out the resources at hand - a costly and unsustainable practice that prevents people from using their capabilities to their fullest.

Optimum is the best use of resources in a way that gives us the greatest degree of value and adaptability possible, while respecting the life of our resources. It is a perspective that grows from being appreciative of the resources we have.

12. LEADERSHIP/MANAGEMENT

We want to respect the profound differences between leadership and management in the growth of an organization.

Communities of work are fields of planned and unplanned events.

There are situations where things happen predictably, largely because they happen according to policy, procedure, or plan. This is the formal side of the community where performance is largely a matter of compliance.

Outside the pockets of predictable spaces we manage to carve out of the organization, everything else happens more spontaneously, improvisationally, and unplanned. Even if we can forecast what might happen in our organization, we may not always be as certain about how and when it may happen. Either because of flexible organizational structures or the intrinsic nature of change, events on the informal side of the organization are not so predictable and can't be handled with predictable policies, procedures, and plans. In the informal spaces of the community, people are more spontaneous, creative, and improvisational.

The intent of leadership is to inspire passion, identify opportunities, and engage strengths for change, creativity, and innovation. Leadership is key to any community's ability to use its capabilities adaptively in new ways. Leadership unleashes new dreams, dreams that go beyond what we've so far imagined possible. Leadership inspires people to dream beyond what they've ever thought possible.

The role of leader is to dream the impossible and inspire the improbable.

Management is the opposite intention - to maintain predictability through the administration of compliance. Management is the administration of compliance to policies and procedures. It is focused on making the trains run on time. When we want the consistency of no negative surprises, management is a tool to make that happen. It is the tool of the formal organization to maintain predictability.

Leadership is about inspiring and engaging adaptive variation, change, and creativity beyond what has already been accomplished through managed compliance. Leadership is the domain of everything in the organization that cannot be predicted or controlled. It's designed to handle things that happen unplanned. Leadership's prime value is in situations outside the box of prescribed behaviors in the organization - in the white spaces on the organization chart where things happen unplanned.

The prime tools of management are instructions; the prime tools of leadership are conversations. The purpose of leadership is to create conversations with an intention to create new ways of combining capabilities for new levels of performance.

Leadership is the domain self-organization rather than management-dependency. Leadership doesn't negate or compete with management. People who have management/leadership positions are often responsible for the paradox of supporting and serving both. Both have their place in the scheme of things.

- *What are things in your organization that require management and what are things that require leadership?*

Deficiency organizations are often imbalanced, heavy with management and light with leadership. In these organizations, people often:

- Pay attention and respond to only what's inside the box of their job manual
- Wait for information, permission, and orders without taking initiative; they do only what they are explicitly told

- Are uncomfortable with ambiguity, lack of clear "direction from the top", and change
- Resist tasks and opportunities that take them outside their comfort zones
- Want everything spelled out in order to prevent any creativity, individualism, or risk
- Hand over problems and decisions for others to take the initiative on - putting the proverbial monkey on other people's backs.

People used to cultures of leadership are more easily present, proactive, creative, and dependable. They self-organize around ambiguity and are agile in response to change.

13. APPRECIATIVE LEADERSHIP

We want leaders who have durable faith in the seen and unseen capabilities of their people.

Appreciative leaders are dedicated to engaging people in using their personal and collaborative capabilities toward the sustainability of the organization.

While deficiency focused managers walk around every day checking to see where people may be failing in their work, appreciative leaders walk around checking to see how people are able to use their best capabilities in their work. The difference in the tone and impact of these two approaches is profound.

Appreciative leaders engage people in new ways because they always expect that people have more capabilities than they may demonstrate at any point in time. These quantum leaders expect to be surprised by hidden capacities. Deficiency managers take the view that what you see is what you get. If people aren't performing to expectation, it proves the presence of capability deficiencies.

Appreciative leaders see it differently. They see performance struggles related to three potential issues:

- People have the required capabilities but haven't yet figured out how to apply them in this situation

- People have the capabilities and know how to apply them but some barriers in the organization discourage or prevent them from doing so

- People haven't yet developed the capabilities required for this level of performance.

When organizations have the courage to change leader-dependent teams into self-organizing teams, they often uncover leadership capabilities in people no one ever knew existed. These are in many cases capabilities people developed in formal and informal leadership roles in their personal life venues. They are capabilities the organization never engages until people are invited to share leadership in self-organizing team architectures.

- *Which teams in the organization might benefit from being more self-organized?*

The leadership paradigm is a self-fulfilling cycle. The more deficiency managers expect people to be deficient, the more they work overtime compensating for the gaps they struggle to decrease and eliminate. The more appreciative leaders expect people to be capable, the more they discover unexpressed capabilities.

14. DYSLEADERSHIP

We want to fill leadership positions with people who have leadership capabilities.

Every organization has stories about people who accepted leadership positions for which they were not prepared. They were more attracted to the rewards of the job than the opportunity for impact they could offer. Parallel stories speak of people who lingered and languished in leadership positions that changed beyond their personal capabilities or the empowerment of the position.

It is no secret that a good nurse, technician, engineer, teacher, sales staff, professional, or manager doesn't automatically make a good leader. Appreciative leadership calls for a specific constellation of qualities, knowledge, skills, and passions that go beyond those required of technicians and managers.

In dysleadership, people in positions designated for leadership fail to provide it. They may provide some level of management or administrative tasks - but not leadership. The most fortunate dysleaders inherit or hire people on teams self-directed enough to effectively compensate for their lack of leadership capabilities.

Dysleaders hurt performance by failing to assess the capabilities of their people and therefore they get in the way of their people's natural capacity for initiative taking. As a result of their lack of trust and confidence, they limit their people's potential for passion and performance in their work and ultimately in their lives.

They provide an imbalance of support - either in non-presence or micromanaging. Micromanaging can emanate from an intention to be helpful, pressure from above, mistrust of people in general, counter-productive perfectionism, or a combination of the above.

Most unfortunately, dysleaders' fear of failure prevents them from sustaining high performance standards. They keep standards unchallenging at a level equal to their underestimating the capabilities of their people. Their penchant for excuse making (and taking) further reinforces messages about their low expectations. In deficiency organizations, their pervasive negativity about people and problems is supported as normative and responsible "leadership."

- *What might help dysleaders discover their leadership passion and capabilities?*

In appreciative organizations, significant intention and attention is paid to preventing dysleadership in the first place. Whenever possible, teams are redesigned to be self-organizing instead of being assigned dysleaders known more for perspiration than inspiration. When potential leaders seek leadership positions, a very full and wholistic mapping of their capabilities and the capabilities of their team guides the process.

When dysleadership becomes an issue, coaching is a useful tool to help struggling leaders discover their passions and strengths. Many people have what it takes to be effective leaders. They simply need the coaching and empowerment necessary to apply their capabilities to their roles.

If enough progress is made, everyone wins. When progress isn't made to the degree that it needs to be, the organization has a social responsibility to liberate anyone from any position that requires more than they are currently capable of providing to that role. The more creative the organization, the more likely it is that the organization can create or find a better position for the person's capabilities.

15. APPRECIATIVE ORDER

We want to trust people's innate appreciation for order in their work.

So, knowing how dynamic organizations and their environments are, how do appreciative leaders help people achieve the kind of consistency required to achieve their financial, operational, and marketing goals?

One of the more ubiquitous success indicators in organizations is people's ability to achieve consistency in outcomes. Our markets reward us for consistency in the look, feel, and function of our products and services. On a cost scale, there is an element of efficiency in consistency.

The creative tension in attaining optimum levels of consistency is that we attempt consistency in a world of ever-shifting conditions, resources, opportunities, and priorities. Paradoxically, consistency in outcome results from constant agility in how we sail toward our mark in this sea of change.

The role of leadership begins with an understanding that *people are naturally attracted to the symmetry of order and alignment.* Even without being over-managed, people seek order in their world.

All of us inherently seek to enjoy and create the beauty of patterns in nature and the rhythms of our lives. It's our natural appetite for order that inspires and sustains our personal and communal habits, norms, values, continuities in priorities and preferences, routines, and sense of organization. It's this appetite that inclines us toward harmony and things that "work."

- *Where do people you know naturally seek order in their life and their world?*

The job of appreciative leader is not to micromanage a set of top-down procedures, policies, and processes to achieve these goals, principles, and beliefs. Their job is to engage people in the self-organization of fluid rules that can support consistency in outcomes.

To micromanage the rules of work is to act as if people do not have the capacity for creating order in the processes and outcomes of their work. To do so prevents people from using this natural, innate capacity and causes people to mistrust their innate capability to appreciate and create order. To do so prevents people from tapping into their natural capacity for the kind of creativity it takes to create consistency in a world of continuous change.

Deficiency managers logically seek to control through micromanaging because they don't understand and appreciate people's intrinsic capacity for order and creativity. When appreciative leaders engage people in leveraging these capacities, people often rise up to the occasion in new, unpredictable, unplannable, and amazing ways. They figure out the best rules for the job at hand.

In complex systems, like organizations and markets, natural order emerges in consciousness and conversations. The astounding dependability of open source technology development epitomizes the magic of appreciative leadership.

Appreciative leaders trust that emergent order occurs naturally in human systems to the degree that they create the space for reflective and generative conversations. Through conversations that are more dialogue than debate, and more creatively collaborative than competitively adversarial, authentic consensus, alignment, and resonance emerges in the community - naturally and without being micromanaged, hierarchically directed, or strategically coerced.

16. PASSIONS

We want to ask people to base their work on their dreams for the best outcomes possible.

Our capabilities are at the root of our success. The heart of appreciative leadership is engaging people in the discovery and use of their capabilities. Our capabilities include our passions and strengths.

Our passions include our interests, imagination, intentions, and principles. Each of these gives us vision, energy, purpose, alignment, motivation, and juice in our life and our work. Our passions take us beyond what's already been done to new possibilities. The more passionate we are in our lives, the less dependent we are on others to lead, motivate, and direct us. The more empowered we are to think, feel, act, and interact in new ways.

Our interests are at the root of our passions. Our interests include everything we're drawn to explore, know, understand, and discover in our work and our life. The more interested we are in our world at work, the more passionate we are. As interests change and evolve, so do our passions.

Our interests define the bandwidth of our attention that fuels and focuses our passions. We pay attention to what interests us. Our life reflects our interests. People bring to their communities an evolving, aligned, and diverse field of interests. The more leaders can tap into these in service of the organization's interests, the more everyone benefits and the stronger the organization and its performance becomes.

Our imagination is the field of possibilities we dream about within the dynamic scope of our interests. They are the "what if" images that attract us, that speak to our hearts and soul. Interests move toward reality through imagination. Imagination allows us to translate intentions into the actions required for manifesting our interests. Passion begins and grows in the fertile ground of our imagination. The richer the field of possibilities we can imagine, the more passion we have for life. Communities that invite people to dream about what the community can be manifest a vitality that lasts generations.

- *What might happen to their energy levels if people in your organization dreamed bigger about what they want for their organization, customers, and themselves?*

Our intentions express our commitment to our dreams. We express our intentions as our wants, needs, expectations, promises, goals, missions, and agendas. Intentions give us the energy, courage, purpose, and commitment to move from dreams to action. Intentions represent what we choose to say yes to in our life and our work. For every yes, we're saying no to countless other options available, and the stronger our no, the stronger our yes.

We make a difference in our world and our work because we have the intention to do so. We design our life and our world based on our intentions about how we want them to look, work, and feel. Intentions help us create the conditions for bringing our imagination and interests to reality.

Our principles include the operating guidelines, truths, beliefs, and values we use as a compass to give our lives direction, purpose, and meaning. They originate from our teachers, spiritual traditions, and life experiences. They are the core beliefs that guide us in our intentions as we navigate through life's continuous changes. Sharing common principles allows a community to act with alignment, resonance and coherence. Even though we may each manifest it in unique ways, shared purpose is at the core of sustainable communities.

Appreciative leaders spend a lot of time engaging people in the communication and alignment of their interests, imagination, intentions, and principles.

17. STRENGTHS

We want people to bring all of their strengths to their work.

Our strengths include our knowledge, skills, personal qualities, and relationships. Each of these empowers and enables us to do what our passions require.

Our knowledge includes our personal, general, and specialized areas of knowledge. It includes accumulated, learned, and real-time knowledge. We gain knowledge from our ability to pay attention to our world. At the root of knowledge is attention. How effective we are in fulfilling our passions, expressing our qualities, and using our skills depends on the knowledge we have. What and who we know drives everything we are able to do.

Our skills include all of our abilities - those we've mastered as well as those emerging and still spiraling in learning curves. Whether we demonstrate our skills consistently or not, any that we demonstrate even inconsistently are skills we have. The only prerequisite for a skill is that we've done it once and still have the mental and physical equipment to pull it off again. Our skills include our technical and social skills, as well as our recreational and personal skills. Skills are gained through observation, practice, and feedback.

Our qualities include the personal characteristics we've accumulated to date through observation, practice, and feedback. They include characteristics like honesty, compassion, perseverance, patience, courage, sense of humor, empathy, male energy, female energy, introversion, extroversion, pain tolerance, risk-taking, focus, loyalty, resilience, confidence, authenticity, optimism, and joy. Whether we demonstrate any of these qualities consistently or not, any that we've demonstrated even once and even situationally are qualities we have.

Our relationships are part of our capabilities because in a changing world, the scope of our performance capacity is directly related to the scope of people we can call on and collaborate with at any point in time. We continuously interdepend on the passions, qualities, knowledge, and skills of others in order to fulfill our passions. The richer our networks and ecologies of capable people in our life, the more we are able to achieve.

- *Where in your organization are relationships that are working and how could they be considered valuable resources and put to work in new ways?*

Appreciative leaders make it their business to keep up to date on people's knowledge, skills, qualities, and relationships.

18. CAPABILITY MAPPING

We want people to understand the depth and breadth of their strengths.

Communities of work thrive to the degree that they utilize people's strengths and passions. If people don't feel alignment between the passions of their organization and their strengths, they do joyless work, which ultimately translates into work that needs to be expensively over-managed. Even then, joyless work that underutilizes capabilities fails to be all it could be otherwise.

The first job of appreciative leaders is to understand the scope of their own strengths and passions and those of their people. Because the organization's performance requirements and people's learning curves are continuously evolving and dynamic, mapping capabilities is an ongoing task.

The mapping process is an appreciative and detailed assessment of our personal and collective knowledge, skills, qualities, relationships, interests, imagination, intentions, and principles. We want to keep updating knowledge and skill directories. We want to keep updating social network maps indicating where key resource relationships and nodes exist. We want to keep updating people's goals in their work based on the dreams they bring about their organization and markets and their innovative and entrepreneurial spirit and ideas.

- *What might be new ways people across the organization can share their goals and competencies?*

The more we understand everyone's capabilities, starting with our own, the more abundant our world appears - and is. The more we can call on these capabilities, the more passion we can cultivate, share, and depend on. The more we can be interested in, the more we can imagine, the more we can be intentional about, the higher principles we can live by.

Mapping is keeping track of the passions and strengths that exist and emerge in a community of work. It's a process of understanding which strengths are well utilized and which are underutilized, as well as which passions are aligned and which aren't. The job of leader is to be a continuous reminder to people about their strengths and passions.

19. No Bad Ingredients

We want to understand our "weaknesses" as strengths used at the wrong time

Inevitably, when we take inventory of strengths and passions, we discover behaviors that don't align with the organization's highest passions - or with people's own goals and principles. People make mistakes, act in self-defeating ways, and create problems. Managers and leaders fail to manage and lead.

We label behaviors as "bad" if they fail to create satisfying outcomes. From an appreciative perspective though, a strength is a strength as long as it's effortless for us, regardless of how satisfying the outcome. Some of us have strengths in procrastination and socializing that can get in the way of our productivity when we employ them at the wrong time. Procrastination and socializing are effective in certain situations and simply ineffective in others.

Performance problems are often not the result of wrong intentions, but wrong timing. Success is all about the right timing of the right resources. Appreciative leaders constantly remind people of just that.

In the appreciative kitchen of organizational performance, there are no bad ingredients, just ingredients that each has unique value in specific situations. Every strength is valuable in some situation. Affirming all parts of us relieves us of the kind of defensiveness that gets in the way of using our qualities in more effective ways. Self-affirmation is the basis of wholeness and integrity.

Sometimes, our situational effectiveness calls for patience, intuition, flexibility, and humor. At other times, it calls for contrasting persistence, data-driveness, firmness, and seriousness. To be skillful as a leader is to have a diverse ecology of strengths to draw on at any point in time. Each strength has its place.

The simplest analogy is not calling a fork a poor performing spoon, nor calling a spoon a poor performing fork. Each tool has its unique strengths and needs to be used in the right situation to do the right job. Neither is deficient in what it is. Both are perfect resources for the right task.

At the root of procrastination is the ability to defer gratification. If we can put that to work where that talent belongs, we perform well. On any given day in project management, there are countless tasks that should not happen until a future date. Appreciative leaders constantly help people remember the capabilities they have that can serve the situation at hand.

Mistrust is a sense of protectedness, which has its place every day in specific situations. At the basis of whining is passion for a better world that if recognized and leveraged, could inspire a new generation of action. Behind the need to control is commitment to excellence that can be framed in a way that inspires courage rather than compliance.

- *What would happen if we could look at all parts of us through an appreciative lens?*

Sometimes it is best for us not to jump into something today; we are better to be data-gathering, analytical, and reflective first. Sometimes we are most effective when we're not as friendly as usual and there is merit to being demanding and unyielding. Sometimes honesty delivered without compassion is not the best course for all concerned. Sometimes protecting others from honesty isn't compassionate and we need to forego their disfavor in sincere attempts to expand consciousness. Good leaders balance the hard and the soft.

No single set of qualities are useful in all situations. Attempts to narrow life down to a few virtuous principles of behavior are helpful for short attention spans but are not sustainable in the long run. In the long run, we need a full palette of qualities to effectively perform in our work and our life. Defining one set of qualities that are "good" and another that are "bad" disables us into being half the people we need to be.

The job of appreciative leader is to help people honor all of their qualities with dignity and worth. This translates into being creative about how each can be effectively packaged and leveraged in the right situations.

20. CULTIVATING PASSION

We want to awaken in everyone their capacity for passion in their work.

Passion is the intersection of our individual and shared imagination, wants, attention, and principles. Passion wakes us up in the morning, gives us endurance in adversity, and inspires us to use our strengths in new ways. Passion allows communities to exceed each previous generation's reach.

Appreciative leaders inspire people to use their imaginations in their work to visualize outcomes that will attract resonant opportunities and capabilities. They engage people in visualizing the details of best outcomes possible in every dimension of their work. They pose the kind of questions that inspire courage and ignite creativity in creating WOW! outcomes. They want people to imagine beyond their self-imposed constraints of fear, caution, and cynicism.

Appreciative leaders are known both for their personal passion and their ability to inspire the passions of others. They ask people to imagine the best possible outcomes for themselves and those they serve. They engage them in conversations where they can imagine the best possible legacy for the organization's next generation of contributors, partners, and markets.

Appreciative leaders help people break free of their fear of dreaming. For those who dream too small, appreciative leaders push the envelope of inspiration past the timidity of their vision of what's possible. They evoke the magic of big dreams.

Appreciative leaders help people get beyond the social myth that the unhappiness we experience when we don't fulfill our dreams is caused by our having big dreams in the first place. They help people understand that when we suffer, it's because we over-focus on what we don't achieve. Big dreams partially fulfilled don't cause suffering.

Deficiency attitudes cause suffering. If anything, people who have unfulfilled large dreams are often more passionate than people with unfulfilled small dreams.

- *What would people dream if they dreamed without restraint?*

Always mindful that an organization is a field of conversations, appreciative leaders take advantage of even the most mundane hallway and watercooler chats to focus people's attention on what they most want to happen in their work.

An important dimension of our passions is our principles. Guiding principles are useful truths based on values. They help us make decisions and assess choices. They inspire us when our energy is low or compromised. They help us navigate through life's inevitable fog of ambiguity, uncertainty, and change.

The clearer we are on our operating principles, the better. The role of appreciative leader is to help people explore, define, communicate, align, and act on their principles. Principles are often statements like:

- People support what they help create
- We tend to be smarter together
- Who you know is as important as what you know

Appreciative leaders are known for the principles that shape their actions and decisions.

21. ALIGNING PASSIONS

We want to create alignment between our passions and the passions of our markets.

Only through coincidence, communication, or collaboration do our individual passions align together in a single coherent whole of intention.

Our passions are naturally diverse and not necessarily connected or cohesive. They can easily be outright contradictory and abrasive. Diverse communities, especially those not yet accustomed to sustainable alignment, can be habitats of competing interests and agendas. To make matters worse, many deficiency organizations are designed with internal competition built into the system - for example, when sales and production departments are divisively incentivised for opposing and competing performance metrics.

Being on the same page is not necessarily a given within teams, across teams, or among leaders in organizations. Our inherent diversity guarantees that we will always have unique passions and pathways to fulfill them.

Cultivating the alignment of passions is key to coherent performance in an organization - each of us performing in ways that create a synergy of strengths rather than competition and disconnects between our strengths.

The first level of alignment in an appreciative organization is the alignment between the organization's passions and its market's passions.

- *Where do your organization's passions align with the passions of its markets?*

If we're a consumer products organization and our market's passion is products that continuously improve in design, recycling-capabilities, and cost, we will be most sustainable when we align with these passions.

The second level of alignment is alignment between the passions of those inside the organization - vertically and horizontally across all levels and functions. This is the work of deciding together what kind of organization we want. The organization's design needs to serve the organization's promises to its markets, its success indicators, as well as the career, work, and life goals of its people.

The role of leader in creating passion alignment is to facilitate regular and ongoing dialogue on the collective imagination, interests, and principles across the organization.

22. KNOWLEDGE MANAGEMENT MYTHOLOGY

We want to understand the role of knowledge in a wholistic way.

Knowledge is one of our core personal resources in sustainable communities of work.

How well we perform as leaders depends both on expert and social knowledge - on what we know and who we know. In the case of knowledge that changes quickly in any field, who we know actually becomes more important than what we know. Other people are our best search engines when knowledge moves so fast we don't even know the right questions to ask.

The role of leader is to participate in the capture, communication, use, and development of new knowledge in all aspects of the organization. An organization after all is only as good as it thinks.

There are three myths that play into sustainable knowledge management on personal, organizational, communal, and global scales.

Myth 1. Wisdom = knowledge

More than ever, organizations want wisdom that's sustainable and appreciative. We can have a boatload of knowledge and very little wisdom. Wisdom is knowing the right questions that tell us what kinds of knowledge are more important than others. Sheer quantity of knowledge doesn't drive success; success is about having the right knowledge at the right time. Having the right knowledge is about having the right questions. A core competency of appreciative leaders is the ability to formulate the right questions.

Myth 2. Knowledge = information

One of the clearest distinctions between knowledge and information is that we can have information we don't understand but we cannot have knowledge we don't understand. Knowledge is information that has meaning for us. We can collect dumpsters full of information and still have little profound understanding of something. Knowledge is understanding - the whole, connected sense we make of data points.

Knowledge is the ability to see the patterns of the dots, not just the dots. It's the ability to constantly see connections between variables, people, and trends. The ability to see the non-local impacts of local actions in a system is an important dimension of knowledge. Another is the ability to see the assumptions driving our actions and decisions.

Myth 3. Knowledge = skill

This is the myth that the more knowledge we have, we more skillful we will become. Knowledge is half of skill; the other half is the mastery than comes with practice. Conceptually knowing how to cook and never spending time in the kitchen effectively prevents the development of the skills required. Knowing leads to doing when knowledge comes from action beyond conceptualizing.

- *What kind of knowledge would truly transform your organization?*

In appreciative organizations, knowledge is respected as one dimension of our capabilities. Knowledge has value to the degree that it helps us develop, use, and appreciate our skills, qualities, relationships, imagination, wants, attention, and principles.

23. DEFINING TARGETS

We want to translate our passions into measurable performance targets.

The more clearly we can articulate in measurable terms what we most want for our markets, our organizations, and ourselves, the more possible it becomes for us to create the conditions for our success.

Performance targets define the scope, speed, quality, cost, and impact of what we deliver externally to our markets and internally to other people who depend on what we do in our organization. We are always defining targets on two levels - immediate and ultimate. The ultimate target is what we optimally want others to have thanks to our efforts. The immediate target is what we're aiming for in the near term.

We may aim for an ultimate 100% on-time delivery in a specific part of the organization, and if we're at 85% now, we may set an immediate target of 90%.

- *How would your organization translate its passions into measurable targets?*

It's important that our performance targets are realistic. In civic communities, the goal of having every child graduating and every parent working may be worthy ultimate and sustainable targets. Immediate targets need to be defined in the most realistic terms possible. Realistic means supported by available capabilities, resources, and opportunities.

Making targets optimally realistic and achievable isn't necessarily about lowering them to the level of our current capabilities. It is always about constant attention to and development of our individual and collective capabilities.

Realistic in the long run means what will bring about the most sustainable success for the organization. A target is only ultimately realistic from a market perspective if it aligns with the market's scorecards - as they are rather than how we might wish they were.

So a performance target of 99% on-time delivery might be realistic from a market perspective and a stretch for us from a capabilities perspective. Appreciative organizations take the challenge because they are masterful at improvising current capabilities for new levels of performance. Their obsession with success inspires confidence that deficiency organizations only feel when the bars are lowered enough to make them achievable based on past performance capabilities.

Appreciative leaders define targets in ways that inspire and engage people to use their capabilities in new ways.

24. COMFORT ZONES

We want our passions to move us beyond the boundaries of our comfort zones.

If we don't lure ourselves out of our comfort zones by dreaming bigger, life will do just that for us. With its intrinsic and infinite appetite for change, our world is constantly moving the targets of our individual and collective success.

Our world raises the bar of our expectations for several reasons. Markets are fields of dreams. Our markets continuously dream of things that are faster, better, cheaper, and easier. They want something new, something fresh, and something that inspires and engages their hearts and imaginations. No matter how committed we are to the cocoon of our comfort, life seeks change.

Another factor is that to those who give well, more is asked of them. It's a universal principle - like the inevitability of earthly gravity and the seasons. The better we do, the more confidence people have in our ability to do more, and naturally the more they ask of us - raising the bar of expectations continuously.

The first appreciative task when we find ourselves outside our comfort zones is to quickly remember that in most cases, we have the strengths required by the situation. Being pushed beyond our comfort zones is no time to wallow in deficiency defensiveness, denial, or fear. It's a time to call on our personal and collective strengths to succeed with whatever we're called to do. It's a time for courage and imagination and calling on our capabilities in new ways.

- *For expectations you now have that are outside our comfort zones, what strengths and passions do you have that can support your adaptability?*

25. Appreciative Accountability

We want to hold people accountable for understanding their successes and the causes of their successes.

In deficiency organizations, we work hard to hold people accountable for their deficiencies - their errors, mistakes, and disappointments. The belief is that fear brings out the best in people. Fact is, fear can provoke compliance, but not creativity. When work calls for any kind of improvisation, fear cripples rather than empowers people to work with the attitude that best supports new levels of performance.

In appreciative leadership, we spend more time working to get people to be accountable for their successes than their failures.

- *Where do you see people attributing their success to factors they consider inside their "control"?*

Holding people accountable for success means expecting people to report on their successes and improvements. It means asking them to identify their personal and collective roles in bringing this about. Appreciative leaders don't let people weasel out of owning responsibility for their improvements and successes with clichéd glossing over the details of their precise role in them.

They also know that without detailed understanding of one's success, all one can do is replicate failure. Getting people to "take the blame" for their success in an appreciative organization is as important as getting people to own blame for failure in deficiency organizations.

26. CAPABILITY TRANSFER

We want to help everyone see that success is about the transfer of existing strengths to new situations.

From an appreciate approach, when current expectations exceed our past performance, our success depends on our ability to transfer the capabilities we have to the new expectations.

When we get a new project that represents new challenges, we need to quickly decide how our current capabilities will support success in this project. This is simply and importantly the work of identifying which of our existing strengths can help us succeed in the situation at hand.

Then our job is to invent ways to apply these capabilities to the requirements of the situation.

- *What kinds of capabilities do we have to meet a new challenge?*

In most cases, we have what it takes to perform successfully to the new expectations. Our lack of clear method or confidence in this success is not an indicator we lack the prerequisite capabilities. It is often simply an indicator that we haven't yet decided: a) which of our current capabilities will best serve these expectations, and b) how we can use these capabilities in our success.

Capability transfer is then a three-step process:

- Getting clear on the expectations we're aiming to achieve
- Deciding which of our current capabilities we'll need to achieve these
- Improvising the new use of these capabilities in service of these expectations

The role of appreciative leader is to facilitate the kinds of conversations that can help people confidently and creatively move along in this process with each new emerging expectation at work.

27. BUILDING STRENGTHS

We want to help everyone understand that they already have what it takes to succeed.

From an appreciative perspective, building new strengths is first and last a matter of using our existing capabilities in new ways.

When we learned higher levels of math in school, we were taught how to use the skills we already had in new combinations and sequences. New levels of performance came from new ways of using the capabilities we already had.

When we learn to use new kinds of technologies, we're simply given new recipes of action and attention that allow us to use what we already have in new ways for new results. When we learn to handle more complex interactions with people, we're simply learning to use the qualities, skills, and knowledge we already have in ways that we haven't before. Good training and coaching simply gives people new recipes of attention and action they can use to employ their existing capabilities for new results.

Cooking demonstrates this well. When we can barely cook, we have all the skills we learned playing in childhood - washing, cutting, peeling, chopping, shaking, pouring, and arranging. When we learn how to master complex new recipes, we use exactly the same skills -- only in new ways with new ingredients and technologies. In the learning process, we gain no new fundamental skills, only new ways of using these skills with new ingredients and technologies.

So from an appreciative approach, building new skills has nothing to do with focusing on what's wrong with us, what we lack, or how we've failed so far. It's all about understanding the capabilities we have and improvising new ways of using them.

- *What strengths do we have outside our work that might have a place serving tasks at work?*

28. ALIGNMENT & CHANGE

We want to understand that success is about alignment.

Our personal performance is at its best when there is alignment between four success factors:

- The total sum of our capabilities
- The way we spend our time at work
- The current goals of our organization and team, and
- Our personal and career passions

Alignment means:

- The strengths required in our work align with the strengths we have
- Our work gives us opportunities to develop new strengths that align with our personal and career goals
- The strengths required for our team and organization goals align with the strengths we have

Alignment is a constant adjustment. Organizations change, their leadership and priorities change, their market pulls and supplier pushes change, the nature of the work changes as technologies change.

- *What new strengths might support people in your organization adapting to current changes they're experiencing in their work?*

We change. Our view of our career path and life aspirations shifts as we transition through learning curves, plateaus, and achievements. New degrees and training invite rethinking our future directions and the strengths we want to develop to support their fulfillment.

Re-alignment at times means renegotiating the scope of our work; trading tasks, responsibilities, decisions, and projects with other people whose strengths better serve them. Sometimes it means adjusting our career goals to better match new competencies we've developed through the natural course of our changing work and organizations.

At other times, alignment means developing new levels of knowledge, skill, or qualities to better serve new requirements in our work. If we work in organizations that are growing or shrinking fast, shifting to new areas of business or mission, our strengths may need to adjust accordingly. Continuous change requires continuous adjustments.

29. AUTHENTIC CONFIDENCE

We want to grow communities of work that empower people with a sustainable sense of self-confidence.

People perform well when they feel the confidence to perform well. Trust in their ability to succeed in their work inspires them to be inventive in the use of their strengths. A lack of confidence leads to hesitation, procrastination, and the kind of second guessing that leads to mistakes. Even when work is done well, a lack of confidence deprives us of joy in the process.

Authentic confidence in performance comes from continuous improvement and mastery that have four requirements.

1. Appreciative feedback

It's the job of leader to do the kind of micromonitoring it takes to catch people doing well in their work. Appreciative feedback is acknowledging how people use their capabilities to handle obstacles and hit targets.

2. Self-critique

The most important critique is our own. Self-critique of good performance is the most immediate and accessible resource in any performance and learning process. Appreciative leaders call on people to rely on self-critique as a prime tool for their continued self-confidence and performance improvement.

3. Opportunities for learning

Emerging and developing capabilities become strengths when we have sufficient opportunities for practice, improvisation, feedback, and mastery.

4. Coaching

Expert and peer coaches draw from the rich source of their experience to give people tips for improvement. Their practical wisdom and appreciative encouragement get people through tight turns on sharp learning curves.

Appreciative leaders know deep down that people perform with heart and consistency when they are confident in their capabilities. Authentic confidence is confidence in the abundance of capabilities that are available for our success. People who work for appreciative leaders rely on the continuous message of confidence, "*I know you can do this*," their leaders covey to them in their work.

- *Where would confidence cause people to perform more skillfully in their work?*

30. UNDERSTANDING LIMITATIONS

We want to engage in work that honors our limitations.

We all have limitations. Things we don't know and can't do. Things we don't dream or have the personal capabilities and resources to support. Things we're not interested in, committed to, or passionate about. Things we don't believe we can achieve.

Each of our capabilities is inherently limiting; each is a boundary of possibility. Each of our strengths allows us to do certain things but not others.

Our limitations represent what so far in our life has been outside the scope of our experience. If you increase your personal capabilities by 100 times today, you would still have an infinite number of limitations. If you started a list of limitations you have today, you could never live long enough to complete the list.

- *What limitations in your organization do people need to honor?*

Limitations are a given for each of us. The issue is not how many limitations we have, but rather what we take on and how this is supported by our capabilities. Integrity in work depends on a deep appreciative respect for our limitations - even in the process of our working to overcome them.

There are two good reasons for us to take on any kind of job, work, project, opportunity, challenge, or relationship: a) because their requirements match our capabilities enough for us to be successful, and 2) because we can use the opportunity to develop new capabilities. Appreciative leaders help people take on work that align with their capabilities. They respect people's limitations as opportunities for both effective assignments and development.

When people are engaged in work not supported by our capabilities, their leaders need to redesign the work, develop the required capabilities, or look for other work. Which option we pursue has everything to do with the availability of resources and opportunities.

The key in honoring our limitations is to say yes to that which will honor the use of our capabilities to create value and develop new capabilities. That's why teamwork is so critical to the success of the organization - because our complementary strengths make individual limitations less relevant.

31. SELF-DIRECTION

We want to create organizations on the understanding that organizations are always self-organizing whether we see them that way or not.

At the individual or team level, the highest level of performance is self-directed performance where people share responsibility for leadership. No one has to baby sit them. They trust their own voice and vision. This trust infuses the kind of self-confidence that allows them to take initiative, act with courage, and give themselves fully to their work.

Though self-directed people don't want to be managed, they love to be appreciatively led. They pay attention to what needs to be done and they do it. They collaborate with people whenever valuable.

- *Where do people in your organization already take initiative and get things done without being micromanaged?*

Appreciative leaders have passion for building a community of self-directed people. They never take responsibility for other people, always expecting other people to be responsible for their own choices and paths. They trust people who have learned to rely on their own eyes and ears to determine how best to serve and collaborate with their community. They know that getting in the way of this is the quickest way to prevent community. At any point in time, appreciative leaders know they are either building sustainable community or preventing it.

Leaders use their questions as the prime tools for facilitating people toward the optimum self-organization they are capable of and that the situation requires. Simply equipped with wise and timely questions, leaders help people use their innate capacity for self-organization in the fulfillment of their highest intentions and dreams.

When people feel ultimate responsibility for themselves, they step up to the task at hand. Only when they believe that other people or some patriarchal or matriarchal culture will take responsibility for them do they fail to take responsibility themselves. Hierarchical cultures are always prone to taking responsibility away from people, and in doing so prevent community that their mission statements speak to.

Appreciative leaders remind people constantly that their life is always their own responsibility, and it is this gift that empowers them to act accordingly.

32. OPPORTUNITY SEEKING

We want leaders to be in constant search and creation of new opportunities to help people manifest their personal and shared capabilities.

Appreciative leaders are in constant search of new opportunities to connect people's passions and engage their strengths and resources. They will create opportunities; they will network to uncover opportunities. Looking beyond the horizon of limitations and constraints, they continuously scan the landscape for opportunities no one is talking about yet.

Several basic questions guide their curiosity and exploration:

- *What more would we want to achieve?*
- *Who isn't yet collaborating, sharing, or working together?*
- *What new ideas need to be supported in the cycle of fulfillment?*
- *Who has resources other people may need?*
- *What kind of space and time seems underutilized?*
- *Who has needs other people may have resources for?*

- *What's already working on a small scale and can be magnified?*
- *What's working elsewhere that we might try here?*
- *What would evoke a WOW! experience in people?*
- *What are people dreaming and not yet pursuing?*
- *Where does there seem to be more talk than action?*
- *What resources and capabilities seem to be underutilized or wasted?*
- *Where might collaboration accelerate results?*

The only limit to our ability to notice and create new opportunities for inspiration and engagement is the scope of our attention and the breadth of our imagination.

- *Where in your organization would opportunity-seeking be a refreshing alternative to deficiency criticizing and complaining?*

There are two simple ways to open our eyes to new opportunities: thinking bigger and thinking smaller. Thinking bigger means exploring opportunities for impact at a scale beyond what we're already considering. It's thinking in global terms - *How can this have reach beyond its existing reach?* Thinking smaller means looking for new grassroots experiments we haven't yet considered or pursued.

The key to opportunity seeking is being fearless in what we dream. It's encouraging people to follow their intuition and excitement about roads not yet traveled, and creating new roads where none existed before. It's paying attention to what calls for new applications of our capabilities and resources. It's paying attention to the impossible and the improbable. It's looking for experiments on macro and micro scales. It's the quantum practice of seeing the universe as it is - as an infinite field of potentiality, waiting to be discovered, created, and fulfilled.

33. APPRECIATIVE FAILURE

We want to totally reinvent how we define and deal with outcomes we call "failure."

In most communities of work, it is easy for people to become nonappreciative about failure. We try new things and they produce less than what we think should have occurred. Every community has stories of events and outcomes that get framed as "failure." The appreciate leader's role is to help people understand their experience of failure from an appreciative perspective.

When life presents us with opportunities, which it does constantly, we have two options - to explore or refuse them. Saying yes to any opportunity is always an act of faith. Life gives us opportunities but no guarantees about their size or complexity relative to our capabilities. We take on new relationships, projects, jobs, and assignments without having the certainty of whether or how success will occur. We say yes betting on the odds we'll have what it takes to succeed. We are better off saying yes than no to life's endless invitations to explore beyond what we have imagined possible - whatever we do or don't achieve in the meantime.

Appreciative leaders help people understand that we need to have bold passions. We need to honor our deep longing to be a part of something larger than ourselves - something that exceeds the apparent scope of our known capabilities. We need to say yes to opportunities and commitments without necessarily the guarantee of outcomes. Organizations grow by taking risks.

Appreciative leaders practice the Open Space Technology principle that in the pursuit of any goal, "the only thing that could have happened did happen." This is not fatalistic, it is realistic. In reality, we always do the best we can based on our opportunities, resources, and capabilities at the time. There is no wisdom in "shoulding" ourselves in the foot believing otherwise. If we want the future to be different, we simply need to seek different opportunities, new resources, or new ways of using our capabilities.

No amount of criticizing ourselves or others will gain us the perspective, passion, creativity, and confidence it takes to achieve better outcomes in the future. The only value past disappointments have relative to the future is their ability to reveal fresh opportunities to use our capabilities in future scenarios.

Appreciative leaders communicate their boldest expectations and requirements effortlessly and unhesitatingly, understanding that it is always somewhat uncertain whether people will be able to achieve or exceed these expectations. Appreciative leaders in fact are committed to passions that they have no guarantees about.

It is important for the vitality of communities that we constantly strive to pursue passions that exceed our past achievements. We need to stop talking about our experiments as failures unless we fail to learn from them. The ultimate failure in any experiment or experience is the failure to learn from it.

That's the appreciative way.

- *What might people in your organization take on if they were less afraid of failure?*

34. THE APPRECIATING LEADER

We want leaders who are passionate about the efforts and achievements of others.

By now you're realizing that being an appreciative leader goes way beyond just praising people. Being life-affirming is at the heart of what it means to be appreciative. People know when they're working for appreciative leaders because their work is punctuated with genuine expressions of gratitude for extra efforts, compassionate acknowledgement of obstacles overcome, and interest in the efforts behind everyday and extraordinary accomplishments.

Appreciative leaders take nothing and no one for granted. Their people don't have to guess whether or not they're appreciated.

Appreciative leaders use every media available to express authentic appreciation because they feel as much pride in the work of their people as they feel pride in their own work. Their capacity for praising others is rooted in a willingness to esteem their own efforts and achievements on whatever scale.

- *What do people most like to hear appreciation about?*

When appreciative leaders make work assignments, they do so after good performance already achieved is proportionately celebrated. With their obsession on what's working and what's going well, they have no problem inspiring pride in work deserving of praise.

They also don't wait for heroics and final outcomes. Appreciative leaders are great celebrants of milestones, small wins, and incremental improvements in the right direction. They do not restrict appreciation to heroic achievements only. They understand clearly how much the momentum of praise for progress adds to long journeys on the way to overarching goals.

Appreciative leaders praise best efforts in spite of uncontrollable conditions. They praise good ideas and collaborations, experiments and learning. Whether their praise is private or public, it is often quick and authentic. They also champion peer praise on every occasion possible. They understand that they are not solely responsible for appreciation; their legacy is an appreciative culture.

35. LEADERSHIP AS A WAY OF BEING

We want leaders who are present, proactive, creative, and dependable.

Leadership is a way of caring about how the organization performs. There are four core qualities that make us effective in our leadership within communities of purpose and place. The more appreciative we are as leaders, the more apparent these qualities are in our behavior and personal brand.

Being Present

When we're present in any situation, we're attentive, curious, appreciative, compassionate, and reality-centered. Staying clear on the difference between what we assume and what we have data for, we consider what we don't know (our questions) as more important than what we do know. Being present is paying attention to life's constant flow of details and patterns. The opposites of being present include being distracted, being attached to positions, biases, and assumptions, being defensive, accusatory, judgmental, critical, blaming, uninterested/self-absorbed.

Being Proactive

When we're proactive, we're taking initiative, always looking ahead in order to be prepared for downstream possibilities. We're not waiting (postponing action) for permission, direction, feedback, initiative, motivation, guarantees, or deadlines. The opposites of being proactive include favoring talking over action, allowing ourselves to be unprepared for the predictable, spending more time fighting fires than preventing them, waiting for guarantees, motivation, or perfect conditions before taking action.

Being Creative

When we're creative, we're experimenting, prototyping, inventing, and tinkering. We're focused on ideal outcomes and we're always looking for new ways to move towards these outcomes. The opposites of being creative are debating options instead of researching or trying them, pushing for either-or and win-lose solutions, assuming some problems will have no solutions, cynicism, hoping the problem clears itself up, rejecting ideas before fully exploring, developing, researching, or testing them.

Being Dependable

When we're dependable, we're honest, transparent, trustworthy, and non-harmful. People can count on what we say and promise. They don't have to guess what we want; they can depend on our keeping them up to date in ways that can and will impact them. The opposites of being dependable are having unspoken agendas, not being honest about our wants and experience, overpromising and underdelivering, not caring if people are suffering, taking a win-lose approach to solutions.

- *How does your calendar reflect your personal commitment to these four key qualities?*

The key to leadership is to know what kind of balance of these qualities any situation requires. This kind of balance involves the cultivation and use of our intuition. Intuition is subtle attention to the needs of a situation. It taps into a seamless blend of hunches grounded in the rich field of our experience and curiosity based in appreciation for what's unique about the situation at hand.

Balanced leadership is leading from the wholeness of head and heart, the reality of data and dreams, and the importance of being for oneself and the other.

36. LEADERSHIP, THE POSITION

We want organizations designed to allow everyone to share in networks of leadership.

In most organizations, leadership is still relegated to specific positions rather than shared by people within and among teams. Although, if teams are designed and equipped to be self-organizing, fewer expensive leadership positions and layers of leadership are necessary to support good performance.

Because trust and initiative-taking are naturally higher in appreciative organizations, fewer leadership positions and levels are required. Skillful leaders can handle larger and multiple teams. When performance systems are well-functioning, the success of teams is even more possible.

- *Who in your organization might blossom as a new leader if they were given new opportunities to share in the leadership of the organization?*

In appreciative organizations, leadership positions are created and maintained around a few key functions and roles:

- Making sure their teams have the information they need to make well-timed, smart decisions
- Making sure their teams are collectively, adaptively, and creatively moving toward inspiring objectives that align with the rest of the organization
- Making sure their teams are well utilizing the capabilities of everyone on each team

Appreciative leaders fill their calendars with conversations with team members, their internal and external process partners, and their customers. They spend more time asking strong questions than taking strong positions. They look for ways to engage and empower people rather than thinking and deciding for them.

37. IMPORTING CAPABILITIES

We want to have a deep understanding of the strengths of those we hire.

One of the most important events in a team and one of the more impactful responsibilities for leaders is hiring new people. From an appreciative perspective, importing the right mix of strengths and passions is critical to team success.

In replacement hiring, we want to make sure the most valuable strengths on a team are replenished. In new position hiring, we want to make sure we've assessed well what new strengths the team and its customers need.

The key is to make sure we're hiring in the right mix of unique and complementary strengths. Complementary strengths help teams stay creative; unique strengths help teams stay responsive.

In the interviewing process, we want to design the inquiry process to assess for each candidate's emerging and developed capabilities, as well as each one's personal and career passions. There needs to be alignment between their strengths and passions and the team's goals. There needs to be alignment between the candidate's learning goals and the job's capacity for giving them the support and opportunities for these.

The most productive interview questions are those that focus on the candidate's responses to actual work scenarios. Knowing a candidate in general is useless. What matters is how they *think* about the specific scenarios that will make up the complex landscape of their work.

People tend to perform only as well as they think. The detail of the inquiry scenarios need to help interviewers assess for the tacit and explicit areas of knowledge, skills, and personal qualities the team needs. Well-designed simulations and tests can help round out assessment of the person's interests and capabilities.

At the leadership level, thinking is everything. We hire the right people for the wrong leadership job if we assume that their having had numerous resume responsibilities and achievements is a clear indication of the thinking that went into leading those efforts and outcomes. Leaders can be attributed with all kinds of success that were actually the result of the capabilities of others.

Work history can be useful information as long as it meets two criteria: a) it is behaviorally detailed, and b) it includes details on the exact contexts where the performance occurred.

Questions about weaknesses need to be appreciatively reframed as learning and development goals, for example: *What new areas of knowledge and skills did your last job help you gain?*, and *What new areas of knowledge and skills do you think this job can help you gain?* People struggling with either question will not fit well with any community of work dedicated to being a knowledge-based, learning organization.

- *Who were your organization's more recent best hires and what indications did you have of their success back in the hiring process?*

38. APPRECIATIVE FEEDBACK

We want strengths-based performance feedback that inspires and empowers.

In the deficiency model of performance feedback, people are assessed in order identify areas of weaknesses. At the end of deficiency performance review processes, the performer is awarded a list of deficiencies to work on.

In the appreciative model, we approach the process from the notion that the greatest opportunities for growth are represented by our strengths and passions rather than our weaknesses. Appreciative feedback inquires into what people are doing well and why, what they've accomplished and what resources supported these achievements. We do not obsess over, much less entertain, responsibility-projection marathons.

Appreciative performance reviews are all about helping people shift their attention from deficiencies to capabilities. All that matters in feedback giving is building people's self-trust and self-confidence that energizes their capacity for self-directed performance success. We want people to walk away with a renewed sense of trust and confidence in the capabilities they have to achieve what they and the organization needs to achieve.

An appreciative process clarifies what goals and standards performers intend to address in the coming review period. This sets the stage for defining what new kinds of performance they might want achieve relative to these goals.

- *What kind of simple and powerful questions help people critique their work in appreciative ways?*

The most important part of the review process is the identification of achievement targets and the capabilities and resources used to reach them. The planning process involves identifying four things:

- The performer's upcoming performance goals
- The success indicators they will use to measure progress on these goals
- The capabilities they will use and develop to achieve these goals
- The resources they will use to best leverage and develop these capabilities

The key is that the process results in performers feeling clear, focused, and confident.

39. GROWTH BASED TURNOVER

We want to understand that turnover is inevitable and base it on the growth of people.

People leave their positions in organizations because of their choice, the organization's invitation, or by management edict.

Because appreciative organizations are committed to the growth of their people and the best use of their capabilities, they view turnover from that perspective. They measure good turnover as people whose leaving adds value to the organization; bad turnover is the negligent loss of people whose leaving deletes value from the organization.

They don't fear turnover by people who have outgrown their jobs. If they fear anything, it's people staying in jobs that they have outgrown or people staying in jobs that have outgrown them.

They help people move from jobs where they are no longer contributing or learning. They redesign work to continuously accommodate the growth of the people in those jobs in ways that add new levels of value for the community. They continuously create opportunities for lattice and ladder growth - horizontal and vertical growth opportunities on the organizational chart.

- *If leaders in your organization expressed genuine interest and support for all of their people's career growth, how do you think people would react and how might it impact the organization in a positive way?*

They look for ways to grow the business' scope of internal and market offerings so people with growing strengths have venues to develop and express these strengths in ways that mutually reward them and the organization.

The bias of appreciative organizations is that they are better off having passionate and growing employees turning over every 3-5 years rather than having growth-averse and stuck people stagnating in jobs for decades. In the appreciative paradigm, the gains outweigh the costs of turnover.

40. LEADER AS MENTOR & COACH

We want to support people's continuous growth with mentoring and coaching.

Appreciative mentors and coaches help people transfer existing capabilities to new situations. They help people invent new behavioral recipes for optimum results.

As leaders engage people in coaching, they want to make sure the organization is designed for optimum performance. This means making sure performance standards are clear, achievable, and known. It means making sure resources, systems, and technologies are adequate or in the process of being improved. It's making sure job descriptions and contracts allow people to be specialists and generalists enough for optimum flexibility in assignments.

In my experience, the coaching process begins with an appreciative assessment of the person's unique areas of passions, strengths, and improvement opportunities. We identify target areas of improvement and the resources we'll use to make progress on them.

I prefer to begin the work with outlining the scope of targeted deliverables, the projected timeline, contact and assignment expectations, and mutual responsibilities in the coaching process.

The prime value from the process is that people develop new ways to use their capabilities in order to fulfill their intentions. Coaching is not a hierarchical relationship of haves and have-nots. We're partners, both gifted with different capabilities. We interdepend on each other, merging and blurring the roles of learner and facilitator.

- *How are passion and humility prime qualities of effective coaches?*

It's a process of self-accountability first and last. When the person being coached is struggling, the coach will use gentle but firm questions and statements to provoke inventiveness:

> 1. *Does it feel like I'm asking more of you?*
> 2. *I will do my best to know your capabilities and base my expectations on them*
> 3. *If I'm not assessing your capabilities correctly, you need to let me know*

When performance isn't up to standards, appreciative leaders spend little time debating reasons. They instead use the yin-yang of facilitation and instruction to help people better discover and use their capabilities in performance improvement.

Appreciative coaches more than anything else want to help people become more self-directed. Helping people become more self-directed in their work involves helping them best use their abilities to be present, proactive, creative, and dependable in their work.

At the heart of appreciative coaching is reminding people of the strengths and passions they easily and naturally forget about when situations engage them in frustration or fear. Coaching is all about helping people remember their strengths and passions. The simple act of remembering any of our strengths is in fact a neurological act that makes more possible our acting out of these strengths. One of the coach's most powerful suggestions is for people to *"Remember a time when ..."* they performed at their best, experienced their work at its best, or used their capabilities in a successful way.

On the mentoring side, appreciative leaders show ongoing and authentic interest in how people want to grow in their careers. They connect people with good models for whatever they are intending to achieve. They care deeply about the passions of their people.

41. LABEL LIBERATION

We want to base our ability to differentiate ourselves in our market on our ability to value the uniqueness of our people.

Labels are time-saving devices. On the upside, they allow us to respond to situations automatically. On the downside, they prevent us from spending time exploring, discovering, and learning anything beyond what we already know. If we get too attached to the labeling of someone as an employee, we stay fairly uncurious about their potentials for leadership. When we label someone senior manager, we may lack curiosity about the unique strengths they bring to the table.

The limitation of labels is that they can obscure our vision of people's strengths and passions beyond those obvious competencies implied by their labels. Labels tempt us to expect that people with MBA after their name are smarter than people with education otherwise. Labels encourage us to believe that people on "off" shifts or "part time" lack the same passion and information as their peers. They seduce us into thinking that people out of town are more talented and knowledgeable than local people who enjoy the same mystique non-locally.

Appreciative leaders practice deep curiosity about the unique talents and passions that may be lurking behind the surface appearance of different collars and cars. People who drive pick-up trucks and Harleys to work may have precisely the same passion, smarts, and creativity as people who drive a Lexus or Volvo. Blue collar people may have the same acute sense of financial and social responsibility as their white collar colleagues.

Appreciative leaders work to liberate the labels they use as well as those that constrain appreciation by others.

In diverse organizations, appreciative leaders make it a point to communicate people's competencies across genders and generations, disciplines and demographics. They work hard to counteract false beliefs and assumptions about what people bring uniquely to the table.

Whether or not appreciative organizations have heavy-duty diversity and disability policies and programs in place, the culture is one where diverse resources are intrinsically appreciated in word and action.

Each of us brings a unique and redundant network of knowledge, skills, and qualities to the performance table. Appreciative leaders make a point to be constantly curious, especially when new people are invited to a team and when people are growing with new learning and opportunities in their work.

- *How could your organization more overtly celebrate, communicate, and play up the value of the diverse and unique strengths across the organization?*

In most cases, we each have unique educational and career paths. We each bring to the table diverse experiences outside of work. Some people bring leadership skills from their faith, civic, recreational, and educational communities. Others bring personal qualities gained through a variety of significant and profound life learnings, transitions, and achievements.

Appreciative leaders get to know people for the unique and common resources they bring. Their role is to provide people with observations, questions, suggestions, and requests so they can have an ever-stronger appreciation for their capabilities, learning, and achievements.

One of the mistakes appreciative leaders work to avoid is making assumptions about people based on their external characteristics. They don't assume men can't listen or women can't be tough. They don't assume that people of the same racial characteristics have the same knowledge, skills, qualities, or passions. They don't assume that people of the same generation represent the same level and scope of capabilities. They don't treat everyone alike who work in the same disciplines in the organization.

Honoring everyone's capability uniquenesses, appreciative organizations have access to far more resources than deficiency-based organizations that miss the richness because they're too busy looking at what's wrong and who's to blame for it.

42. Best Use Of Time

We want leaders whose use of time aligns with their passions and strengths and those of the organization.

As much as we try to plan for every event and contingency in our work and life, every day is a constantly shifting landscape of the planned and unplanned. As proactive as we can attempt to be in our work, life sends us all a steady stream of unplanned and unpredictable requirements, information, changes, opportunities, and distractions that require our wise response and reaction.

Whether we're being proactive or reactive, we are at our best when we feel like we're making good use of our time. At these moments, there is alignment between our passions and strengths, the passions and strengths of our organization, and the passions and strengths of our markets.

In appreciative organizations, there is an expectation that *everyone* will take personal responsibility for continuously assessing how they use their time. The essential question driving this inquiry: *Is this task/project at hand a good use of my strengths and does it serve the highest purposes of my life and the life of the organization?*

When requirements and organizational resources change, so must our use of time. When we want to improve any aspect of performance, so must we improve our use of time. How we use our time is one of the most profound indicators of how well we are empowered, aligned, and appreciative in our work.

- *How could you give less time to low-yield time uses in your work and shift that time to higher-yield activities, interactions, and projects?*

43. CONSENSUS BUILDING

We want leaders who are skillful facilitators of appreciative consensus.

One of the principles of sustainability in any kind of ecosystem like an organization is that sustainability requires diversity. Sustainable organizations are always seeking and celebrating diversity of strengths and passions. On most days, getting people on any same page is nothing less than a miracle.

Conflicts and differences are more inevitable as the organization grows. All living systems naturally evolve toward more diversity and differentiation. To resist this is equivalent to resisting the rotation or gravitational pull of the earth.

Healthy organizations are rich tapestries of people who are different. There are the filers and the pilers, the predictability-loving stasists and the change-loving dynamists, the planners and the improvisers, the lone rangers and the collaborators, the protectors and the disrupters, the mission focused and the profit focused, the deficiency-based and the appreciative.

We differ on where we should be going and how we should get there. We disagree on how much risk we should take on and how many opportunities we should pass on. We disagree on how long to keep low-performers and how honest to be with our employees, leaders, customers, vendors, and board. From an appreciative perspective, differences are not signs that we're dysfunctional, disrespectful, uncaring, or permanently divided. Differences are the essential nature of caring, intelligent human relationships and communities.

- *How could we help people stop feeling defensive for their differences? How could we help people to articulate their wants at higher and higher levels until common ground is reached?*

An appreciative approach to consensus building starts with consensus on the highest level of common purposes possible. This itself is not always an easy task but is essential to any further progress. This is the work of identifying our common wants and crafting common dreams.

Once we decide on whatever common intentions we can, we then want to explore which of our unique and collective strengths can be put to work in service of these spaces of intentional common ground.

From an appreciative perspective, consensus has nothing to do with one side of a difference coercing the other sides into compliance. Consensus building is agreement on common purposes and how we can together use our strengths to fulfill these purposes.

Consensus occurs when there is resonance among people's perspectives and passions. Authentic dialogue - based on creativity and curiosity - is the basis for the resonance of passions and the alignment of capabilities in the manifestation of these passions.

44. Appreciation & The Management Of Change

We want leaders who thrive on change.

Change is a constant in all organizations, whether they are dynamically growing, declining, or flat. Change occurs within organizations as long as change happens outside them. Change is not necessarily a sign of the chaos that comes from mismanagement.

Even though the goal of management is to create predictability, the universe is inclined to keep things churning in new ways. At the level of quantum consciousness, life is a verb; nouns are illusions.

- *What changes are inevitable in your community of work and how could they represent new opportunities for gain rather than loss?*

On the list of things that are prone to continuous change are: changes in markets, technologies, economic conditions, legal and political landscapes, and social trends. These changes are a challenge because they often represent changes in performance requirements beyond the capabilities and comfort zones of people. Every change is an opportunity for appreciative leadership.

There are several tactics appreciative leaders consider when helping people respond intelligently to changes that happen inside and outside the organization.

- *Coaching* - helping people use their current capabilities in new ways to meet and exceed the new requirements

- *Hiring* - hiring in new capabilities to help teams meet new performance requirements

- *Outsourcing* - sending work with new requirements out to vendors and suppliers who have the necessary capabilities

- *Partnering* - partnering with other organizations who have the complementary capabilities to help achieve the new requirements

- *Acquisitions* - purchasing new organizations who can meet the new capability requirements

Each tool has their place in the scheme of intelligent and sustainable responses to change. Whatever tool we employ, the key to successful change on any scale in organizations is to engage people's strengths as fully as possible.

When it comes to change, people tend to resist what they don't help create. And the more people are engaged as participants in the ongoing innovations across the organization - in the form of small continuous experiments - the more resilient, receptive, and creative they are when change happens *to* them

45. THE LEADER'S LEADER

We want leaders who are more passionate about collaboration than hierarchy.

In many organizations, people in leadership positions report to people in other leadership positions. There is no limit to the numbers, levels, and areas of leaders and managers in organizations. It is possible to have too many leadership positions. If leadership is more a situationally-focused function and shared responsibility, there cannot be "too much leadership" because people would only exercise leadership in the specific situations requiring it.

Creating new leadership and management positions is a classic tool of deficiency organizations. Positions proliferate to the degree that more positions don't clear up problems.

The solution of more managers or leaders is unsustainable as a deficiency strategy since it rarely improves things in an enduring way. More leadership and management positions draw leadership sharing away from people, lowering their initiative taking, creativity, intuition, and confidence - only making things worse. Usually only budget constraints limit the endless proliferation of leaders and managers.

Appreciative organizations are designed for shared leadership, where leadership is more distributed to where the real work occurs. Instituting more leaders to "manage" existing leaders is resisted in favor of better assessing, leveraging, and developing the leadership capabilities of people and teams doing the organization's work.

- *How could your organization better utilize the unique talents of leaders who tend to micromanage or neglect the leaders that report to them?*

Where leaders report to other leaders, these relationships need to be designed more as partnerships than hierarchies. In these partnerships, leaders collaborate in the sharing of information, responsibilities, and decisions across vertical and horizontal boundaries, territories, and silos. They leverage each leader's unique perspectives and strengths in service of commonly defined and aligned goals.

Ultimately, senior leaders are measured on their ability to help middle level leaders succeed in inspiring the passions, discovering opportunities, and engaging strengths of the people they work with.

46. LEADER AS STORYTELLER

We want leaders who are good at virally infecting people with passion through skillful and appreciative storytelling.

Appreciative leaders are consummate storytellers. They inspire with stories; they align with stories. The live by the mantra that a single story can celebrate the victory of strengths over the possibilities of defeat. A single story can inspire and evoke more passion than a thousand policy and procedure manuals.

Stories are the currency of appreciative leaders. Stories remind us all - at a visceral level - of the passions and strengths we have that at times can be obscured by times of fear and frustration.

Organizations are the collective expressions and sum of their stories. Every day, people across the organization are crossing chasms, overcoming obstacles, and doing small heroic acts that have unpredictable non-local and non-linear impacts.

Organizations are sustainable to the degree that their markets have good stories to tell about them. Every brand is a story; every achievement and milestone marks the momentum of stories told and untold.

Every untold story of success is a new opportunity for energizing everyone's appreciation for their talents and passions. Every story told empowers and inspires us to use what we have for the greater good of the organization and our greater good.

- *What successes in your organization haven't gotten around to the whole organization yet - and what media might be useful for spreading the word?*

At the heart of the leadership role is the role of storyteller. If you're a leader and you don't think storytelling is a strength, your success will depend on your ability to develop and master the skills and qualities of good storytellers.

The process of cultivating this capacity starts with listening to good storytellers through events, books on tape, conference speakers, and friends. Mastery continues with sheer practice. Starting small, we can gradually increase the length, complexity, and intensity of stories. The other role of appreciative leaders, just as important if not more so, is getting people to tell their success stories in as many venues as possible.

47. LEADER SELF-CARE

We want leaders who do enough self-care to sustain strong energy levels through times of challenge.

Appreciative leaders have their energy challenged and potentially depleted every time they interact with unappreciative people in their world. They daily row downstream against the rocks and undertows of deficiency cultures.

Sustaining and growing one's capacity for appreciation requires constant self-care. This can take as many forms as we have the opportunities and imagination for.

As appreciative leaders, we want to regularly spend planned and serendipitous time with people who inspire new energy with their perspective, compassion, and humor.

We want to spend time in spaces and activities so compelling that while we're there, we completely forget about our work and our selves. This can be working out, being in nature, or being involved in some activity that provides a "flow" experience where we get so engaged, we tend to lose track of time.

We cannot sustain appreciation if we allow our energy to go out of balance in favor of depletion. No one but we can take the time to take care of ourselves so our energy stays strong and positive.

- *What reenergizes you? Where do you go to be nurtured and refreshed? What needs to go on your calendar that aligns with your intention for self-care?*

48. THE INNER GAME OF APPRECIATIVE LEADERSHIP

We want leaders whose appreciation at work is simply an expression of an entire lifestyle of appreciation.

We lead the way we live. Our capacity for appreciative leadership depends on our practice of being appreciative in all other aspects of our lives.

The appreciative perspective as daily practice means being very intentional about where we focus our attention and how we spend our time. It's being appreciative about our own capabilities, celebrating our own successes, and focusing on what works and why. It means engaging people in talking about what's going well, what they want, and what's improving.

The appreciative lens is a challenge if we've been accustomed to the gravitational pull of deficiency cultures that keep us focused on what's wrong with ourselves and our world.

Appreciative leaders don't passively allow their attention to be shaped by deficiency-focused people or conversations. They know that appreciative attention is the root cause of sustainable value for themselves and everyone they engage with. Their passion is to help people become more appreciative themselves.

- *If you practiced making a daily list of what you're grateful for, what would be on your list today?*

So appreciative leaders discover that they want to practice appreciative attention in all aspects of their lives. In accidental conversations with friends, family, colleagues, and strangers, appreciative leaders help organize the collective consciousness around that which affirms everyone's best.

They spend time keeping up with new resources, projects, and relationships. Their questions focus less on negative gossip and excuses for insufferable whining and more on what people most want for themselves and their world. They spend personal time daily meditating on the objects of their gratitude.

For these leaders, appreciation is not just a way of leadership; it is a way of life. It is their practice in life that supports their impact as leaders.

Appreciative leaders are effective to the degree that they personally practice what they preach. They continuously work on defining their own personal sustainable passions and develop their own emerging and mature capabilities. It is this commitment to personal practice that makes their leadership authentic and effective.

49. APPRECIATIVE ORGANIZATIONAL DESIGN

We want to design every aspect of organizations from an intention to unleash passions, strengths, and opportunities.

Performance is a function of design: things tend to work the way they're designed to work. This is true whether we're talking about technology, environments, or organizations.

In communities of work, design is the interplay of intention and practice within the natural conditions evolving inside and outside the organization. On the intention side, we design the physical spaces, configurations of technology, communication systems, formal policies, procedures, and processes. On the practice side, organizations form from the quality of conversations that make up the quantum matter of organizational ecologies and habitats.

Deficiency organizations design themselves around the problems, fears, and weaknesses of people. Designing for deficiencies often means costly and restrictive over-sight and corrective mechanisms that can feel more punitive and non-trusting to people inside the organization.

In deficiency organizations, we see enough layers of management to act as speed bumps for real innovation and empowerment. We see people arranged in boxes of functional silos and job descriptions in order to prevent unplanned interactions, with the hope that more planned interactions will result in less chaos for managers to manage.

Appreciative design is based on the trust in and development of people's strengths and passions. Appreciative organizations tend to design self-organization into the functioning of teams on all levels in all areas.

People tend to be more cross-trained and assignments are more flexible and based on strengths rather than weaknesses. People are less micromanaged and therefore managers have more time to be leaders. Leaders have more time to be proactive rather than always fire-righting and crisis-management reactive - both of which constrain leaders from using their best strengths in their work.

• *What might happen to the physical and process look and feel of the organization if your organization was more designed around people's strengths and passions?*

In deficiency organizations, the role of boss is designed as manager rather than leader. Manager-heavy organizations leave little room for the kind of spontaneity, self-initiative, and creativity to warrant leadership. Manager-dominant organizations are designed to divide everyone in two classes of power and information haves and have-nots as a means of maintaining compliance and predictability through control.

When bosses are more leaders than managers, people act with more of the self-confidence, trust, agility, and creativity it takes to use their best talents to fulfill their highest dreams and the dreams of the organization. High levels of performance depend on high levels of authentic trust of leaders. Appreciative leaders easily cultivate and win this trust.

The most sustainable, smart, and adaptive organizations are networked rather than hierarchical organizations. Things get done in self-organizing networks rather than rigid reporting structures. The wisdom of networked organizations is based on a few key principles:

1. When information, knowledge, and wisdom are dynamic, who we know at any given time becomes as important if not more important than what we know
2. The more people are connected - especially informally - in a network, the faster and more accurately communication occurs across the organization
3. The better people are connected, the better resources are utilized and opportunities discovered
4. The role of leader in networked organizations is to facilitate new connections and new levels of conversation for resource, knowledge, project, and opportunity sharing.

Perhaps the more sustainable feature of networked organizations is that they are interaction and project driven rather than institution and hierarchy driven. This feature automatically gives organizations an adaptive edge in dynamic and complex environments.

50. CREATING A CULTURE OF APPRECIATION

We want leaders who know how to foster a culture of appreciation.

In an appreciative organization, culture is the sense of freedom people feel in their work. In appreciative cultures, people feel more free than constrained in pursuing their dreams as they align with the organization's dreams.

- *In your organization, do people on all levels feel free to dream and use the best parts of themselves in their work? Do they feel free to learn and contribute, and to move on whenever they're no longer learning or contributing? Do they feel free to be innovative and to participate in the decisions that directly shape their performance? Do they feel free to have new conversations among themselves and the people they serve?*

A culture of appreciation is not accomplished through programs, speeches, presentations, or email edicts. People tend to resist the patriarchal or matriarchal coercion of conversion. They push back on even well-meaning attempts to take responsibility away from them.

A culture of appreciation is not achieved through fear-based harangues or lectures. It's not cultivated through warnings or whinings about the problems we're "still having" as if we will ever be problem-free.

Whether or not the sponsors, funders, or shareholders of an organization feel socially responsible for the legacy of capabilities currently supporting organizational performance, the organization's appreciative leaders will always act with passion for creating a culture of appreciation.

Creating a culture of appreciation is achieved through appreciative actions. Appreciative leaders thank people for doing a good job - *especially* when it's expected of them. They want people to understand that good performance through the best use of their capabilities is always a choice they make situation after situation, day after day. They make sure people celebrate successes and milestones.

Appreciative leaders are continuously monitoring areas of common learning across the organization and work to create and support informal, self-organizing special interest groups and communities of practice so people can share in support of each other's learning intentions.

They help people communicate, connect, collaborate, and coordinate through the use of open-source online environments, especially when these environments can facilitate the archiving and accessing of knowledge as it is created in the organization. They help people rely on the organization's social and knowledge networks for learning and coaching.

Appreciative leaders make sure people have opportunities to participate in projects that stretch the development of their knowledge, skills, and qualities.

51. INTRINSIC & EXTRINSIC APPRECIATION

We want leaders who help people practice self-appreciation in everything.

In the inner game of appreciation, we can only feel as appreciated by others to the degree we appreciate ourselves. If we don't appreciate what we do, the appreciation of others will have only limited and certainly not sustainable value. No amount of external appreciation can be a sustainable substitute for internally-driven appreciation.

Appreciative leaders put a premium on helping people appreciate themselves for their contributions, impacts, and steps toward any kind of improvements. Before becoming the extrinsic source of positive judgment, appreciative leaders encourage people to assess their own performance against standards. Accurate and appreciative self-assessment is more sustainable in the long run.

- *How could leaders help people who feel least appreciated to communicate more about their work's achievements and successes?*

So how does this relate to formal rewards and recognition programs and informal acts of appreciation? Appreciative leaders pass by no opportunities to use whatever media and events possible to send people messages of appreciation, in general for their contributions, and especially more specifically for unique contributions.

Media include kind words in private, words of praise in front of others, emails, notes, cards and other symbols of appreciation. Celebrations around food and beverages go a long way to communicate authentic appreciation because it is personal, significant, and often memorable.

Appreciative leaders create a culture where 360 degree appreciation is expressed - vertically and horizontally, internally and externally within and outside the organization. They apply their creativity in engaging customers and clients as prime sources of appreciative feedback - sponsoring surveys, focus groups, conferences, events, and inviting them to formal and informal recognition venues.

52. STRENGTHS BASED TEAMS

We want strengths-based teams.

Appreciative teams strive to make sure people have work that achieves two intentions:

- Each person's work uses their best strengths and aligns with their highest passions
- Each person's work gives them opportunities to develop new areas, applications, and levels of strengths to serve their passions and the passions of the organization

Appreciative teams keep track of everyone's shared and specialized areas of knowledge, skill, and qualities. They keep an updated directory of these so everyone who interacts with - and joins - the team can know the scope and depth of resources on the team. Appreciative teams also make sure there is some level of understanding about everyone's personal passions.

The team's leaders make sure there is updated information on the organization's passions - translated into measurable goals. This task is not exclusively the domain and responsibility of the team's leader; the leader's job is to help the team share this responsibility.

Appreciative teams make sure the design of work aligns with the strengths and passions of the team members and the organization. Where strengths are diverse, people are assigned to tasks, responsibilities, decisions, and projects that align with these strengths. Where strengths are common and redundant, assignments can be rotated and shared.

In an appreciative organization, the issue of pay differentials can be separated from the architecture of work assignments. The organization can choose to differentiate pay on education, experience, and specializations related to the organization's core mission and competency requirements.

But when it comes to the assignment and doing of the work, the constancy of change in any organization requires that the team's highest level of performance will be driven by the most flexible assignment model possible.

When a team is appreciative, the team doesn't need to be restricted by imposed job descriptions. The assignment of tasks can be flexible, fluid, and responsive to changing conditions and competencies. In the best case, assignments are designed collaboratively.

In an appreciative culture, the most flexible model of work assignment is built on two rules:

- Whoever is most available and able to do something is the best person to do it
- Whoever starts something is the best person to finish it

So as in some hospitals, in the UK for example, you can walk into a patient's room and see anyone from volunteers to physicians to administrators making a bed. You may see a nurse aide or surgeon starting an IV, but only surgeons doing surgery.

- *How could job descriptions be liberated in your organization to address all of the unplannable and unpredictable events, issues, and opportunities that come up in people's everyday work?*

In this model, the team may agree that there are some tasks that some people should not take on unless they're the most able and available in that situation. This makes them available for doing the specialized and unique tasks only they can perform for their team.

The team may also agree to allow people who are developing new strengths in certain areas to take on the tasks (often with coaching from the more qualified) that will help them develop these areas of new strength. The more common areas of strengths across the team, the most flexible the team is in responding to work as it changes.

53. The Entrepreneurial Organization

We want organizations known for creating entrepreneurs.

Growing up, some of us managed and co-managed summer lemonade stands, paper routes, and garage sales. Today, we barter goods and services in our neighborhoods and help our children peddle sales to support school projects and trips. We help our communities of faith with fund-raising events. Some of us had entrepreneurial parents, teachers, or mentors who passed along their passion and mindset for marketing and business growth. In our careers, we've all had to re-brand, re-package, re-price, and re-distribute our talents for new positions

We all come to the table with entrepreneurial spirit, appetite, and abilities. Appreciative organizations acknowledge this and leverage it for mutual gain of the employees and the organization.

There are multitudes of ways organizations can tap into the entrepreneurial talents of its members. They can engage people in the research and development of new lines of business, product lines, markets, programs, and services. They can engage people in marketing and selling its offerings through the development and participation in their natural social, communal, and professional networks. They can invite people into the continuous innovation of new possibilities and improvement of existing processes and systems.

- *What might be some interesting entrepreneurial opportunities for people inside your organization?*

They can offer organizational resources to help people create unique civic and economic development partnerships within their professional and social networks.

Some innovative organizations position and design internal teams and departments as internal vendors to the rest of the organization they support. They frame their interactions with internal currencies and contracts, expecting that these support units can grow into self-sustainable *intraprises* - and sometimes enterprises to customers and clients in the marketplace.

In the most innovative organizations, support teams are encouraged, incentivised, and structured so they can take their core competencies to the marketplace as entrepreneurial organizations. If an organization excels in the way it delivers training and media services, it might help its training and media team market these competencies to customers outside the organization.

Every time a team or department is empowered to act with some level of vendor autonomy, all the while aligned with the organization's goals, the people in those areas use a higher level of capabilities than their peers who work in more constricted structures.

Everyone wins in the intrapreneurial and entrepreneurial models. Intra/entrepreneurial employees increase their strengths and extend the scope and impact of their passions. External success complements and infuses greater passion for excellence inside the organization. The organization increases its revenue and brand reach, making it more sustainable than ever.

54. THE POWER OF THE INFORMAL

We want organizations who foster informal environments to cultivate their rich network of relationships.

It's easy for many organizations to romance and idealize the role of leader. Traditional folklore has it that unless people have a strong leader, they wander in an aimless and chaotic lack of productivity and non-alignment with the rest of the organization. This will happen, but mainly in deficiency-based and management-heavy environments that have prevented the democratization and development of leadership.

When we consider the traditional role of leader, we realize how much of the leaders' power was based on their privileged and often exclusive access to knowledge. Knowledge made the difference between the leadership haves and have-nots. In this model, without exclusive knowledge, the "leader" has no power to effectively lead.

Today, with the unleashing of social and technology networks, we are seeing the democratization and dynamic distribution of knowledge. Leaders no longer have exclusive domain over knowledge or the passion fueled by it. In fact, an informal, virtual network of people can have more shared up-to-date knowledge about almost anything than any single unconnected leader could ever have.

The informal networks of people that make up organizations are the informal, unlegislate-able, dynamic ecologies of relationships based on the sharing of knowledge, resources, and opportunities. In a connected world, anyone with knowledge is a leader. Leadership as an institution of exclusive knowledge becomes extinct in a connected world.

Leadership in a connected world is transformed into a way of being and interbeing where freedom in our connectivity allows us to become partners in sharing response-ability for processes and outcomes through the sharing of knowledge.

The informal side of the organization is the ecology of knowledge-sharing and innovative interactions that are unplanned and spontaneous. The informal organization energizes the capacity for people to have conversations at watercoolers, after meetings, in the hallways, through weblogs, instant messaging, and phone calls.

- *How could your organization foster what tends to happen naturally in the informal side of the organization?*

Most new and useful learning happens in the informal organization where people get new ideas in conversations with available experts and peers. In real-time informal interactions, people tend do get their most practical and sustainable learning because it is specific, immediately applied, and yields immediate feedback.

The more that appreciative leaders promote informal access to expert coaching and information, the more freedom people have to improvise with their current resources and build new strengths.

One effective approach to promoting the informal organization is to provide people with electronic and online media where expert information can accumulate and be accessed when learners want it. The more knowledge, tips, and short cuts can be archived and accessed 24/7, the more sustainable they can be in long term service of people in the future of the organization.

In business and life, so much of what we are able to do is linked inextricably to what and who we know. Social and knowledge equity on some days trumps economic capital.

Everyone in our lives interacts with us within in a social habitat of 3 dynamically interdependent social circles.

- People in your 1st circle are people you know well
- People in your 2nd circle are those you know, but not well

- People in your 3rd circle are those who are in your 1st and 2nd circle's 1st and 2nd circles

According to social network anthropologists, we tend to interact most naturally with people like us. We have a built-in affinity for people like us - people who know what we know and who we know.

The further out we go in our circles and connect with people outside each circle, the more likely we will connect with people and knowledge that will be new for us. And through these people and knowledge, the more likely we will connect with opportunities that will be new for us.

And since there are only about 3-5 people between us and almost anything we want for a good life, and given that everyone's relationships and opportunities are always changing, everything we want is always somewhere within the reach of our dynamic and abundant circles. Appreciative leaders live in an abundant world knowing this, and help their people see this abundance through this lens. Our social connections fuel our creativity, passion, and impact.

55. APPRECIATIVE ORGANIZATIONAL IMPROVEMENT

We want to base continuous improvement opportunities on the passions and strengths of people.

One of the limits on engaging our capabilities in our work is the design of the organization. All organizations are designed in ways that constrain people's ability to use their capabilities in new and effective ways.

Organizational design includes:

- How processes are designed
- How physical layouts are organized
- How technologies work
- How information and communication systems operate
- How decisions are made
- How performance standards and feedback are communicated

When these variables are not well designed, they get in the way of people being able to use their strengths to fulfill their passions and the passions of the organization.

An appreciative approach to organization improvement begins with data-based and systemic mapping of what's working well in these areas and why. We can skip wasting time in deficiency mode. It then involves defining what we want in the future, and how we can best use people's strengths to create improved design in the areas that can make things faster, better, more efficient, or easier. This is creative and innovative work that requires collaborative efforts by those with situational and expert knowledge and skills.

- *What organizational design improvements could make it more possible to use their best capabilities in their work?*

Organizational learning is then driven by the team's dedication to the research and testing of new approaches. One of the prime criteria for improvement is that people feel like their strengths are better utilized in the process and make a larger difference in the outcomes.

56. THE PARTNERSHIP PARADIGM

We want to understand that partnership relationships outperform customer-supplier relationships.

Whether organizations think of themselves as service, product, or technology businesses, everything they produce to their markets is delivered through some kind of service relationship.

In hierarchically cultured organizations, service relationships are unilateral. One person is there to serve another in an unequal balance of knowledge, expertise, power, or responsibility. In partnership-oriented organizations, the service hierarchy is replaced by a partnership relationship focused on mutual service for mutual satisfaction.

The partnership model is the most sustainable because it calls forth the collective strengths and passions of supplier *and* user. Wealth creation is all about the creation of appreciative partnerships.

- *Where would it make sense to reframe traditional internal customer-supplier relationships as partnerships based on the mutual sharing of information, resources, and responsibility?*

Appreciative leaders tend to favor partnership relationships because they leverage the resources of both supplier and user. Appreciative leaders engage people in the mutual sharing of information, responsibility, and decision in every possible service relationship and transaction.

Knowing people support what they help create and that we're smarter together, appreciative leaders help people feel free to share initiative taking. They know that distributed and collaborative decisions are often faster and actually less risky than when made by managers isolated by their blind-spots, egos, or political firewalls.

Making the transition from a hierarchical to partnership approach happens in phases. It takes education, a different set of metrics, and different fulfillment and delivery systems. Because a service partnership is based on mutual service and satisfaction, it calls on the mutual sharing of capabilities, resources, and responsibility among everyone in the service network.

57. THE LEARNING ORGANIZATION

We want to create learning organizations.

Business publications frequently feature stories of organizations that wake up successful 5 years after a crisis because they developed the capabilities to take on more robust and sustainable business approaches.

In some cases, they take on new lines of business that represent the development of whole new design, financing, and fulfillment competencies. In other cases, they represent innovative deliverables and competencies in the organization. The appreciative organization stays passionate about learning because learning drives the organization's capacity for renewal and transformation - vital qualities in constantly changing political and economic conditions.

Appreciative organizations move their learning forward through formal training, informal coaching, hiring in new knowledge and abilities, and creating communities of practice around emerging and developing practice competencies.

- *What would it mean for your organization to become more of a learning organization?*

Appreciative leadership is vital to learning because all learning has learning curves - zigs and zags in and out of performance failure and success. As every craftsperson intimately knows, learning creates as much waste and scrap as it does value. Evidence of learning progress is the gradual decrease in waste and increase in value.

Learning is at root the new application of existing strengths in the service of new intentions, goals, and purposes. As appreciative leaders, we help learners with the endless improvisation of existing strengths required in every new learning process.

The best learning is a movement toward new desired outcomes rather than movement against unwanted outcomes. The deficiency perspective doesn't accelerate learning; if anything it discourages it, prevents it, and makes it more difficult than it needs to be. Weaknesses play no role in the learning process. They are naturally transcended in the use of existing capabilities in fresh ways.

58. COMMUNITIES OF PRACTICE

We want to create micro-communities where learning can thrive.

One of the more effective tools for advancing organizational learning is the community of practice. A community of practice is an informally structured, evolutionary group of people who share common concerns, problems, or passions in a way that deepens their knowledge, expertise, connections, and collaborations

There are several possible kinds of communities of practice.

- **Helping Communities**: Participants engage each other in their respective projects/problems

- **Best-Practice Communities**: Participants develop, validate and communicate/publish best practices within their domain

- **Knowledge-stewarding Communities**: The community hosts forums for members to organize, upgrade & distribute everyday domain-specific knowledge so more people have access to it as it evolves

- **Innovation Communities**: The community exists to be an incubator to new ideas and initiatives

A single community of practice can take on single or multiple intents, further divide into sub-communities that take on specific intents, and can shift from one kind of intent to another.

There are 3 key elements to any community of practice:

- **Domain**: The shared passion that energizes and organizes the community
- **Community**: The people, activities, resources, events, communication tools, membership renewal and development
- **Practice**: The knowledge, learning, and innovation created, distributed, and developed by the community

Communities of practice can be self-organizing or leader-directed. The role of the community includes:

- Identifying key issues related to the domain
- Facilitating community events planning
- Informally linking people & resources
- Nurturing participant development
- Helping build the practice: knowledge, tools, methods
- Monitoring and facilitating the community's culture

- *What kinds of communities of practice already exist informally in your organization, and what kind of learning interests do people share that might be able to inspire new practice communities?*

59. APPRECIATIVE SUCCESSION

We want to continuously cultivate the next generation of appreciative leadership.

In their passion for creating value for future generations, sustainable organizations are always looking ahead to the next generation of leaders. It matters deeply to them who they cultivate and support today to be leaders for tomorrow.

This is no small task in this world of unpredictable economic, social, and technology changes on local and global scales. Preparing tomorrow's leaders from within the organization's emerging pool of candidates is a task vital for the organization's sustainability. It begins with the organization's clarity about the kind of value it wants future generations to have. Without this clarity, it becomes impossible to define the leadership necessary for it.

- *What would you include on a list of desirable qualities and competencies for the next generation of leaders in your organization?*

Succession planning is not necessarily about preparing specific people for specific future leadership roles. In a dynamic organization or even relatively static organization in dynamic markets and economic ecosystems, this may not even be practical or wise.

Appreciative organizations use mentoring, whether formal or informal, as a key tool to help people in the organization discover and define their passion for future leadership. Appreciative mentoring helps people understand their leadership capabilities and pay attention to opportunities to engage and develop these and other new leadership capabilities.

Developing, emerging, and new leaders will succeed to the degree they have core leadership capabilities. These include passion for leadership, leadership qualities, knowledge of the organization and market, principles that support appreciative leadership, and leadership skills.

Core capabilities are those that can support leaders in any part of the organization, regardless of functional scope or level on the human resource chart.

Effective leaders need both generic core capabilities as well as any specific to the disciplines they support. Because they are members of multiple teams and networks, they need to complement the specific competencies that support and surround them.

From a succession perspective, having a pool of leaders ready for leadership roles for project, operational, and administrative opportunities is critical to the sustainability of the organization's vision and mission.

60. The Future Of Appreciative Organizations

We want to expect that appreciative organizations have unlimited potential.

Communities of work are rich opportunity spaces that invite us to pursue our passions and fulfill our dreams. They are the spaces where we can experience how the power of *we* trumps the power of *I.*

We spend most of our conscious lives at work and derive much of our life's sense of purpose there. Why shouldn't communities of work be deep sources of appreciation for our passions and strengths? Why couldn't they be significant opportunities for our experience of wholeness, authenticity, and vitality?

Those of us who participate in the leadership of our organizations have daily opportunities to practice an appreciative approach. We have endless opportunities to help people appreciate their strengths and align their passions with the organization's and their markets' passions.

We are just beginning to glimpse the possibilities of appreciation. We are just beginning to practice the courage to let go of deficiency models that obsess on what we don't have and what's not working. We are just beginning to empower ourselves with appreciation as a way of living in abundance on this planet.

On the quantum scale, our potentials are ultimately unknowable. Through our work and the communities we create from our work, life invites us to experience this abundance. May we live in and be continuously renewed by a deep appreciation of the capabilities we are.

APPRECIATIVE LEADERSHIP FAQ'S (FREQUENTLY ASKED QUESTIONS)

What about problems - certainly we have to focus on our problems in order to improve performance?

Whatever we consider a problem in our community of work, it represents something we don't want that is happening or something we want that isn't happening. A problem is what's wrong.

What matters from an appreciative perspective is that we define what we want as clearly as we can and mobilize our capabilities and resources in the context of an opportunity as quickly as we can.

People are late coming to work, responding to customers, delivering on promises and projects. These are problems. The appreciative leaders who want more on-time performance know that to end with success, they have to start with success. They talk to people about their people's intentions around being on time.

They ask them to identify where there may be opportunities to be more on time. They ask them to talk about the many instances and situations where they're on time and why. They get people do drill down to the specific kinds of attention, intention, and actions that contribute to their on-time capabilities. They then work with people to get creative about how to use these capabilities in the opportunity spaces they have for being on time.

They follow up with people, micromonitoring the opportunity spaces to catch people doing things right and coaching to support improvements. They are walking reminders to people that they can do what's required and how well they do this. Their people feel immensely supported by them.

This is not rocket science. It's simply being appreciative.

Focusing on problems is good in theory but presents two sharp downsides. In deficiency cultures, it postpones the definition of wants, opportunity discovery, and capability mobilization. People instead squander valuable time and energy doing the requisite whining, blaming, complaining, evading and unrealistic demanding that comes with a problem focus.

The other downside is that problem areas sometime represent low-return opportunities. There is no sustainable value in pursuing small annoying problems instead of larger creative opportunities.

From a marketing perspective, an organization can tinker with all kinds of internal problems that add little or no value to the customer's overall experience of joy. In doing so, the organization prevents the kind of creativity that can instead produce the kind of WOW! experiences that evoke far higher levels of customer joy and loyalty.

What do we do with managers who find it difficult or impossible to be appreciative?

Remember that for many managers who are being asked to make a transition to appreciation, this is asking them to do something radically uncomfortable for them. Our comfort zones are built up over time through our beliefs and behaviors, and are reinforced by the dominant beliefs and behaviors of our communities of purpose and place.

For people who like to feel a sense of control, their control boundaries are equal to their comfort boundaries. The further they are asked to move beyond their comfort zone, the more loss of control they experience. The way control works is that when people perceive a loss of control, they tend to automatically try to hold on even tighter to any control they have. Their breathing restricts, restricting their scope of attention, creativity, and behavioral flexibility. This makes everything more difficult than it needs to be. They become more demanding, less adaptable, and generally unappreciative on every level.

The first task of any community - whether it's a work, civic, social, or faith community - that has deficiency managers is to start interacting with them in an appreciative way. It's uncovering the passions behind their fears. It's catching them doing well and getting them to get in touch with the wealth of their strengths. It's engaging their capabilities where they can best serve the community.

It's then a matter of making sure these managers are increasingly acting as appreciative models of performance, interaction, and growth.

We have to remember that people who come from a deficiency base of fear have the ability to dream and remember their capabilities as much as their appreciative peers. They are just not used to dreaming and engaging in appreciative ways.

What if people have a different vision than their managers and leaders of where they want the organization to go?

When an organization's culture has been predominantly hierarchical, it often has a history of not engaging people in sharing vision-creation. When managers exclude people from vision creation, they unwittingly create the conditions for fragmented, weak, and conflicting images of the future. If managers further allow the division of information of haves and have-nots when it comes to marketing, financial, and technical knowledge, they invite divisions in vision about the future of the organization.

Creating vision alignment requires nothing less than ongoing knowledge and dream sharing. If the conversations are reality-centered (data-driven) enough, convergence of vision becomes more possible, creative, and sustainable. If the conversations are more dialogue than debate and more inclusive than adversarial, the more possible it is for alignment of passions about the organization and its future.

We understand that self-organizing teams may be more appreciative than leader-dependent teams, but why do so many organizations fear them because they didn't work in the past?

Many organizations experimented with self-organizing teams when they became the next new management fad in the 1990's. Many failed and were abandoned because they were attempted in the unsustainable organizational ecologies of deficiency cultures.

Self-organizing teams only work in an authentic culture of appreciation. Otherwise they do struggle and fail to reach their performance potential. They cannot grow in organizations that are dominated by manager-dependent hierarchies.

Successful self-organizing teams are developed by appreciative leaders who institute appreciative structures and practices in the process of designing the team's organization. They are authentically empowered to create the alignments, goals, and rules they need to succeed as a team of people who share leadership.

How long does it take for an organization or community to transition from a deficiency to an appreciative culture?

People dedicated to creating appreciative cultures tend to passionately work toward creating them whether the work takes months, years, or generations. They favor persistence over patience and creativity over rigid consistency in approach.

With daily practice, authentic intention, and enough emotional support, we as human beings can make significant changes in our beliefs and behaviors in about 6 months.

Several things accelerate the learning curve when it comes to learning how to be more appreciative as an organization.

Increasing the sharing of power and information between the haves and have-nots helps. Increasing the visibility of performance success numbers helps. Making sure all new leaders are far more appreciative than deficiency focused helps. Training and coaching current managers, leaders and leaders of leaders in appreciative leadership helps. Involving people in the defining of performance goals and metrics helps. Increasing the organization's deep knowledge about its markets helps. Fostering a culture of innovation and creativity dedicated to WOW! experiences for customers helps.

The more hierarchical and deficiency-focused the organization has been, the longer the transformation will take. The more class divisions between information and power haves and have-nots there have been, the more creativity the process will require. Teams empowered to be self-organizing that are used to top-down direction won't be self-organizing until they are given the right coaching and training to be. Deficiency managers won't become more appreciative until they get the right coaching and training to do so.

In the end, it matters less how long the transition takes. What matters is the passion with which we embrace every opportunity to take steps in the direction of appreciation. Ultimately, the organization's tendency toward appreciation will self-organize into a sustainable momentum of success.

Good Reads

A growing list of reads that inspired *Appreciative Leadership* and give more depth to some of its core themes

- *Accidental Conversations* / Jack Ricchiuto
- *Appreciative Inquiry* / David Cooperrider & Diana Witney
- *Cultivating Communities Of Practice* / Etienne Wenger, Richard McDermott, William M. Snyder
- *Emergence: The Connected Lives of Ants, Brains, Cities, and Software* / Steven Johnson
- *Expanding Our Now: The Story Of Open Space technology* / Harrison Owen
- *Flow: The Psychology Of Optimal Experience* / Mihaly Csikszentmihalyi
- *Instructions To The Cook* / Bernard Glassman & Rick Fields
- *Leading Self-Directed Work Teams* / Kimball Fisher
- *Now, Discover Your Strengths* / Marcus Buckingham, Donald O. Clifton
- *On Dialogue* / David Bohm
- *Presence: Human Purpose & The Field of the Future* / Peter Senge
- *Stewardship* / Peter Block
- *Synchronicity: The Path Of Inner Leadership* / Joe Jaworski
- *The Power Of Mindful Learning* / Ellen Langer
- *The Web Of Inclusion* / Sally Helgeson
- *Turning to One Another: Simple Conversations to Restore Hope to the Future* / Margaret Wheatley

For the rest of this growing list, visit www.AppreciativeLeadership.org

ACKNOWLEDGEMENTS & HOPES

I am deeply grateful for the people who over the past several years contributed to my understanding and practice of appreciative approaches to sustainable communities of work.

I am grateful to my first circle of appreciative friends, mentors, and colleagues: John Allen, Lois Annich, George Nemeth, Adele DiMarco Kious, Valdis Krebs, Bill Lawrence, Ed Morrison, Bill Doty, June Holley, Bill Warner, Tom Cutolo, and Mel Edmonds. Over the years they have given me unconditional support, enduring inspiration, and immeasurable kindness.

I am grateful to David Cooperrider for his visionary work in Appreciative Inquiry and Harrison Owen for his visionary work in Open Space Technology. I am equally grateful for inspiration from thought leaders Peter Block, Meg Wheatley, Bernie Glassman, and Sally Helgeson.

Finally, I am grateful to the many clients who have inspired me with their passion for and practice of appreciation, too many to name.

To all these people, a heartfelt thank you for adding to my capabilities that continue to serve organizations with sustainable appreciation.

My hope is that every community of work embraces appreciative leadership as the key to sustainability. My hope is that we carry these lessons from our communities of work to our other communities of place and purpose. Doing so means nothing less than the fulfillment of our dreams and potentials on this planet. Doing so means nothing less than the fulfillment of our destiny as stewards of this magnificent planet we have been gifted with.

Thank you!

Jack Ricchiuto
November 2004

ABOUT THE AUTHOR

Jack Ricchiuto is an independent corporate coach, author, and principal with Smart Meeting Design. For over 25 years, he has been serving organizations across 20 + industries, from *Fortune 500* to start-ups. The focus of his work is helping teams and leaders improve their performance through better use of their strengths and resources. His client list includes Ford, MCI, American Greetings, Parker Hannifin, Phillips/Nuclear Division, Viacom, American Institute Of Banking, Doty & Miller Architects, and University Hospitals.

Author of *Collaborative Creativity*, *Accidental Conversations*, and *Project Zen*, Jack has written for national publications including *Projects@Work* and local publications like *Smart Business News* and *Cool Cleveland*. A member of the Society of Professional Journalists, Jack also is a writer conference seminar presenter and speaker.

The core of Jack's corporate coaching work is coaching executives and project teams in performance improvement. His work with Smart Meeting Design is facilitation with organizations and teams and coaching them in the use of collaboration technologies. An early technology adopter, Jack helps client organizations with intelligent and agile use of new tools to support sustainable growth.

With an undergraduate degree from John Carroll University and master's degree from Goddard College, Vermont, Jack continues to teach Executive MBA classes as well as design and deliver seminars in personal, team, and leadership development across industries.

You can visit Jack @ www.DesigningLife.com